CW01499105

INTRODUCTION

A couple of years ago I was in Spain working with a team of Ugandans and some other British people on a Parish Mission. As part of the mission we visited families in the area. I went into one house with the interpreter and it was breathtaking, open plan living area, furniture of the top quality. The woman who lived there was waiting for us with her two children and the husband joined us later. They were lovely people. He had a great job working all over Spain meeting interesting people. She was equivalent to a local councillor and worked long and hard for the community but when I looked into their eyes and got behind the laughter I could sense a real poverty, a poverty of the spirit. As we talked and shared they were fascinated by what had brought me and why I was a Priest doing what I do. At one point the man said to me, with anguish in his voice, 'You don't really believe in God do you?' It was almost as though despite all they seemed to have, they were desperate for something more. I realised they were desperate for life, real inner life. I could understand something of what he was saying because I too long for real deep inner life.

Lately I am aware that within me there is a growing desire for more of God. I don't quite know what that means but I sense it within myself. I am unsettled and want more. I was recently speaking at a local gathering near where I live and the man who introduced me said that every day he woke with a hunger in his heart for more of God. That is the sense I have for myself and I do know it involves the Greek word metanoia which we translate as 'repent'.

'Meta...what?' you might say. Metanoia, a key word in Christian vocabulary that so many of us misunderstand because of the translation as 'repent'. We have traditionally seen repentance as something we do and something that involves sin. The more I reflect on the Greek word metanoia and get a sense of what it really means, the more convinced I am that metanoia is not something I do. It is something God does in me as I am led deeper and deeper into the mystery of love and mercy. The only thing I have to do is be open to metanoia and let it happen. Let love flood me. Let mercy wash over me let the compassion of God change the very essence of who I am and how I make sense of life. That it will change me, free me, liberate me, I am certain but I am equally certain it does not depend on me and it has little to do with the amount of sorrow for my sins that I might have.

Metanoia will happen in the very stuff of life because that

Meta... what?

First published in 2014 by
New Life Publishing, Luton,
Bedfordshire LU4 9HG

© Chris Thomas

British Library Cataloguing in Publication Data
A catalogue record for this book is available
from the British Library

ISBN   978 1 903623 90 9

All rights reserved. No part of this book
may be reproduced, stored in a retrieval system,
or transmitted by any means – electronic, mechanical,
photocopying, recording or otherwise without the
prior written permission of the publishers.

Unless otherwise stated Bible references are
from the New Jerusalem Bible, Darton, Longman
and Todd, UK (1985) and the New Revised Standard Version
Bible: © 1989, 1993 the Division of Christian Education of the
National Council of the Churches of Christ in the United States
of America. Used by permission. All rights reserved.

Typesetting by New Life Publishing,
Luton, UK www.goodnewsbooks.net
Printed and bound in Great Britain

Meta...what?

BY
CHRIS THOMAS

With love and gratitude to Archie and Cathy
and their children and grandchildren
who have shared their lives with me
and allowed me to do the same with them

CONTENTS

**Fr Chris Thomas is the Director of
The Ireneaus Project**

The Project is an attempt to highlight the
whole area of spirituality, not just for those
who can afford the luxury of a Retreat Centre,
but also for those who can't.

He works all over the Archdiocese of
Liverpool with a small team and also further
afield to help people have opportuities to
pray and explore the Scriptures, reflect on
what it means to be human and alive, and
know the truth that God is with us.

is where God is. Life will change me and transform me if I am open to those things that life brings me and if I am willing learn from them. Prayer will transform me if I allow myself to fall in the ever-open arms of God. The Scriptures will be a tool for metanoia if I can ever see them as something more than a moral handbook.

This book has been in my head for a long time and like my other books it is not a theological treatise but a reflection on a word that I think is crucial to understand on our journey into God. I hope you read it with an open heart and mind and wherever you are in your life I pray that it will take you a little further into the depths of God.

CHAPTER ONE

TURN AROUND

Many years ago I worked with a man called Hughie. Hughie worked for an organisation called Youth for Christ. He was a Glaswegian with the sort of sense of humour which comes from those who live in the big ports around the United Kingdom. Like many people born in those areas life had been hard for him when he was growing up. Hughie often said he was poor without knowing he was poor. His background meant that he had to learn how to survive and so he was able to cope with most things that were thrown at him particularly from disaffected young people. I never found out what it was that led him to become a Youth for Christ worker although my own experience tells me it must have been the grace of God.

He had a fund of magic tricks that he would use to catch young people's attention and then when he had their attention he would begin to talk about Jesus. He always finished with the same words. 'You know Jesus Christ was either deluded, a con-man or a fraud. If he wasn't any of those things then he was who he said he was. If he was who he said he was then

are you willing to let your lives be changed by him?'
Transformation is at the heart of the Gospel message but
what is it to be transformed and what might that mean
for us?

In recent years I have been at several gatherings where the
impetus has been towards repentance with a very narrow
understanding of that word. God will respond to us if our
lives are squeaky clean seems to be the underlying
philosophy. For centuries people have interpreted the
Gospel in a very narrow moralistic way. It has been about
right and wrong, good and bad, sin and judgement. It is
not that those things are unimportant but there is always
more. It seems to me that we can undervalue the very real
challenge we have in the Gospels to deep radical
transformation with a superficial doffing of the cap to real
change.

Many people have a developed a sort of Uriah Heap
attitude to God where we keep our heads bowed and
continually say that we are sorry in the hope that God will
forgive us. I sometimes think that to keep saying sorry for
our sins and lack of response to God can be a way of
avoiding real change. With a great deal of willpower and
strength of mind most of us can change aspects of our
lifestyles. That again can be a way of sidestepping the real
issue of the God given fundamental inner revolution that
we are invited to experience.

Richard Rohr the American Franciscan says 'Many people are incapable of true repentance because they are trying too hard. They get into breast beating and putting themselves down. It will never work only deaden and paralyse. That's never God's work. God enters into our sin and redeems us.' The truth is we are forgiven so the challenge is to turn towards the light of forgiveness. We don't have to earn love. It is simply poured out upon us. The invitation is to turn towards love and let it flow through you healing transforming and freeing.

To turn around and face the light, letting go of our need to control takes us into another realm where it is God who does the transforming. You are being called to realise your dignity. When you are in the process of transformation you know who you are. You know that you are a child of God. You understand that you are loved beyond your wildest imaginings. You know that it's got nothing to do with you but everything to do with a God who pours out love. You understand that because of that love you have a dignity and value that no-one can take from you. Your well being is not dependent on what others think of you or whether you are at the centre of everything but on God and God alone. That is where transformation leads you and it will take you further into a deep love for the world and for others.

I am not a Greek scholar and I am well aware that others could write about this far more eloquently. The word that the Gospel writers use when talking about this whole area of change conversion transformation is metanoia. Most of us in Christian circles will have heard of that word without really understanding what it means. We translate the word in most contemporary Bibles as repent with all the overtones of sin and the need to change that the word repentance has.

The process of metanoia is all about what God wants to do within us not about what we want to do for God. I learnt that lesson very powerfully through an elderly lady. For most of my life until she died Teresa was a dear friend of my family. She was born at the beginning of the last century into dire poverty living in one of the courts of Scotland Road. She was one of nine children and money was tight. Her father presented himself every day on the docks to be picked for work but that seldom happened. Her mother scrubbed floors to try and make ends meet.

Teresa left school at 9 and worked on the markets to try and bring money into the family. Despite her hard life her whole existence was centred on God. She did not have a theology degree. She would not have known what theology was or what a degree was but she exuded God and was so 'in tune' with God that she knew beyond doubt that she was forgiven for her failures and loved completely and unconditionally. She would often say in her later years with a smile on her face 'It is all about God, it is all about God.

So what does this word metanoia really mean? Again I have read from people much more qualified than I am that metanoia comes from two Greek words 'meta' and 'noia'. The word 'meta' is translated in English as meaning after or beyond. The English word metamorphosis is used for deep foundational change for example where a caterpillar becomes a butterfly. There is a massive difference between the two. The caterpillar becomes a butterfly and is totally unrecognisable as the caterpillar it was. That is the meta of metanoia. It is a change in the essence of who we are.

The word 'noia' comes from the word nous which I have read is a philosophical concept and refers to the basic building blocks of your life. What is it that makes sense of your life? What are your philosophies about life? What are your gut reactions? How do you live socially politically and religiously?

With that sort of understanding you can maybe get a glimpse of what Gospel metanoia is all about. You move from a caterpillar to a butterfly. You go through a radical metamorphosis. It begs the question are you willing to turn towards the light and let it shine in every area? Your very being is transformed and you therefore live with a different understanding of life and of the world. I hope you can see that it is far deeper than constantly saying sorry and that it never depends on us but on God.

Those who are followers of Jesus are called to metanoia, to that sort of conversion experience that changes us radically and enables us to help others see a God who is alive and who is always surprising.

As I travel throughout the United Kingdom and meet many people I find that I very rarely come face to face with people who are wrestling with metanoia. I think most of us are so egotistical that we find it difficult to see anything beyond ourselves or can even imagine that we need to change radically. Jean Vanier in his book community and growth says 'if we are to grow in love, the prisons of our egoism must be unlocked. This implies suffering, constant effort and repeated choices.' I do not meet too many people who have allowed the Spirit to change them so radically that their hearts and minds become bigger and they can embrace otherness and love the broken and the poor without thought of themselves. Many of us who say we follow Jesus have in fact arrived at a place where we have become narrower in our outlook and more insular towards those who do not live as we expect them to.

The sort of people who are entering into the metanoia process are always attractive to be with, although because of their openness and thirst for God they can be scary people and usually they are seen by the wider Church and certainly wider society as the lunatic fringe, those who have religious mania. They don't live in the real world.

I have been blessed to meet several of those sorts of people down the years. When I was 17 I found myself in Dublin where I met a man called Keith. He was someone who lived for the Gospel. With a steely eye and a commanding voice he could prophetically cut through much of the nonsense we surround ourselves with. At the same time he had a glint in his eye and wicked sense of humour. He was both gentle and strong and had a disarming vulnerability about him. He loved life and the world and everything for him was gift but he hated with a passion anything that destroyed people's dignity or the world we live in. He had long ago given up control of his own life and had stepped outside many of the systems that we so often think we need. He and his family lived by providence and as he put it 'God always shows up' He made me uncomfortable and challenged me to be more open to God, to face the light.

Thomas Moore, who is an American psychotherapist and philosopher, says that metanoia is the process by which we enter into a new world of meaning where our task is to live in a world that is charged with the grandeur of God. Richard Rohr, the American Franciscan, talks about our 'living in an enchanted universe.' The Spirit of God has been given to lead us into a deep place of radical conversion where we begin to see completely differently than we might have done otherwise and realise the truth of God's presence in every individual and all around us.

The questions that matter for those of us who follow the Jesus way are questions like these. Is the process of transformation happening within us? Is the power of the Spirit at work changing us? Is the power of the Spirit freeing us so that we can see what God is doing? Where in our lives are we learning how to love? Are we inviting God every day to melt us and mould us and fill us and use us?

So where does all that leave us? I hope a bit shell shocked but open to finding the more. As yet I haven't mentioned the Kingdom of God, that paradoxical reality that Jesus talked of so often. If you look at the Gospels you will find that metanoia is the key by which we enter the Kingdom of God. So if we do not begin to enter into this process of radical change then we have not encountered the kingdom and I hope that as followers of Jesus to experience that Kingdom is what we want more than anything else. It is certainly the state of being that Jesus wants us to live in as he called it the pearl of great price.

While we might want the Kingdom we have sometimes reduced it to being about religious practice alone. I do not think anyone is to blame for that. For many people their upbringing equated Christianity with religious practice obligations and duties. It is just that there's more and the more is to enter into the metanoia process.

We can go to Church and engage in all the religious practices we want to. We can live moral virtuous lives and fulfil everything that is expected of us. But if we do not escape from the systems that we put into place which give us our security and our identity we have failed to understand what the early Church means by the word metanoia. If we do not begin to think and see in another way then the sad indictment on us is that we have missed the place where the Gospels are pointing us and life will be less than it could be.

CHAPTER TWO

FROM PARANOIA TO METANOIA

A couple of years ago I went to spend some time with a friend of mine who is a Palestinian. He lives in East Jerusalem. We spent days wandering around the old city stopping at various religious sites drinking coffee and just generally sharing about life. I love the city of Jerusalem with all its vibrancy and colour and I was taken to places that I would never have seen had I not been with my friend. It was for me a very blessed time as I was able to share some of my deepest fears and dreams and have them accepted without condemnation.

One day I was on a minibus travelling with six Palestinians and an evangelical American who spoke Arabic. We were going to a funeral on the Mount of Olives. I had been invited along by my friend just for the experience. He said that it would be worth going just to see what it was like. The funeral was very different to any I had attended previously, and very moving too, but it was what happened before it that had a profound effect on me.

The traffic was horrendous and sitting in a jam a conversation began as it always does in that country about the rights and the wrongs of the Israeli Palestinian conflict. I had nothing to say because I don't live there and have no experience of life there on a day to day basis but I found the conversation fascinating and they were good enough to speak in English so that I could understand. I guess they wanted me to feel their pain and understand their position and where they were coming from. One of the Palestinians was quite vociferous about the wrongs that the Israeli's had inflicted on his people and he kept talking about what 'they' had done. This went on for some time with other interjecting about the pain that they felt in being marginalised and discriminated against. Suddenly one of the men who had been silent for the whole conversation cut in and said 'who is this faceless 'they'? There are as many good Israeli's as there are bad Palestinians.

That caused uproar for a few minutes. I think everyone on the bus disagreed with him apart from me and he was shouted down and we slowly went on our way through the traffic with the conversation taking another turn. I have thought about that conversation a lot since it happened. It would be easy to get into the rights and wrongs of the Israeli Palestinian situation but that is not the purpose of writing. The argument that ensued that day stirred something within me. I realised how easy it is to scapegoat and blame particularly in bad situations when it is easy to see the rights and the wrongs rather than to stand in love and hold the tension.

I have borrowed the title of this chapter from a recording I heard of a talk given by the Canadian oblate Ronald Rolheiser because it seemed so apt. Without moving towards metanoia we remain in our paranoid defensive state where we blame judge and refuse to allow others to grow. That can never bring life to ourselves or other people. I have been told by a friend of mine who has suffered from paranoia that when she is ill she can only see negativity and darkness but when she is well and able to look at things from a Gospel perspective she sees only possibility and potential.

I often think as a Church we have to re-learn the Gospel lessons of acceptance and inclusion rather than the rejection and scape-goating that we seem to do so often these days. I find myself wishing for the openness and excitement of the years after Vatican II when we opened the windows of the Church and let the fresh air in. I long for the return of the realisation that we were to enter into dialogue with those who thought differently and lived differently than we do. I hope that we remember the call the council gave us to serve the world rather than to exist in a bubble seeing the world as a bad place. I look forward to the time when the essence and the spirit of Vatican two re-emerges and scatters the climate of fear and darkness that we have lived in for some time. That way of living is so much more life giving than looking at groups of people and naming them as intrinsically disordered or even evil. As a Church we need to move towards metanoia.

On a personal level we all judge others and condemn others usually on the most superficial criteria. We don't like the way in which someone lives or the way they dress or the sound of their voice. Sometimes it's the colour of their skin or their nationality. We look at another person and focus on what we see as negativity within them rather than looking for the good. I have often wondered why that is and have come to the conclusion that it is far easier to judge someone else than face our own need for transformation

Richard Rohr in his book 'The spiral of violence' says: 'Until we can experience the reconciling of the seeming opposites and the mass of contradictions that we are, we will continue to live a split life and we will inevitably be accusers. The negative energy inside of us has to go somewhere. You will tend to hate another race, reject another religion, or fear another country. You have to. I am not saying you might. If you are a split person, I'm saying with 100% certitude you will be an accuser, you will be a blamer, you will be a fearer, and you will be a hater.'

In recent years I have become very aware of the level of intolerance that we have towards one another and the innate inability to accept difference that seems to lie in all our hearts. It seems as though as individuals, and as nations we have to have someone to blame and point the finger at. I think it is probably the cause of much of the violence in the world.

My awareness of these issues has been increased because of various situations I have found myself in where I have marvelled at some people's small mindedness and defensiveness. That has made me take a long hard look at myself and I have recognised within myself that I have a need to embrace otherness and not be afraid of it. I have recognised again that I have to experience the conversion, the metanoia, that the Word of God calls me too, so that I become a reconciler rather than an accuser. Somehow within me that miracle has to take place where I no longer feel the need to divide and separate. Somehow the Spirit has to set me free of own fear of others and my need to be right and others to be wrong when that is simply a way of building up my own ego. Deep within the Spirit has to plant the seed of love that can grow and enlarge my heart. I need metanoia rather than paranoia.

What does metanoia mean if not that our hearts are to become bigger and we are able to accept one another with all our differences and love. When we turn around and face love it sweeps away our need to defend ourselves and attack others. That doesn't mean we have to accept everyone else's point of view nor does it mean that we have to let go of what we hold to be true but it does mean that we have to be big enough to love people whatever their viewpoint. Just recently I listened to a woman telling a story about sitting in a doctor's waiting room. She said that she sat down next to a heavily pregnant Moslem woman who at first would not meet her eye and was obviously anxious and frightened. The lady telling the story said that eventually the woman realised that she was no threat and that they began to talk about the baby who was coming and somehow they forged a bond as they shared love and friendship in a doctor's waiting room.

Our shared humanity has to unite us rather than divide us. It is then that we have the ability to enter into dialogue with people to share the Gospel with them and enable them to grow a little more. As long as we dig our feet in and use those words that so often fall off our lips 'I'm right and your wrong' then we fight a losing battle and everyone simply remains entrenched where they are. In order to show the world how to deal with external conflict we have to learn how to deal with the conflict that arises within. The invitation Jesus gives is to be people who are willing to face ourselves and work through the issues that arise within us so that we have no reason to accuse blame or scapegoat others for the very things that we push away within ourselves.

We can play very successful games with ourselves as we deny our shadow side. Our shadow side is that part of ourselves that we deny or neglect, that which we reject or repress in order to show to others what we see as a more perfect or acceptable image of ourselves. It is our darker side, or perhaps our blind side. We could not possibly be jealous or angry or bitter – could we? To deny it or repress it can lead to catastrophic results, which is beautifully illustrated in the classic story of Dr Jekyll and Mr Hyde. Somewhere deep within ourselves there needs to be metanoia so that we can be reconcilers.

Any spiritual growth is only measurable by our willingness to grow as human beings and that only comes about by increased self awareness, by beginning to accept and face the shadow side. The way I see it holiness is not about kissing the altar rails and saying prayers and knowing all the Church rules. It is about moving towards wholeness spending time with ourselves and allowing God the space to move within us. So that the miracle of transformation that we're all called to experience happens within. Some of the holiest people I know have little to do with Church life but they know deep within themselves the miracle of transformation, people like those on the 12 step programmes who have tasted their own negativity and have allowed it to be touched and changed by their 'higher power.' They are holy people. We certainly don't have the monopoly on holiness and it has little to do with what many of us think it is about.

It is when that process of metanoia happens within us or is happening within us that we will have the courage to bring into the light areas of conflict and disagreement with others and find a way to resolution. It's then that we will be ambassadors of reconciliation and show the world that there is another way to live than the way of violence and aggression.

When I look at the Gospels I discover that Jesus had to face the comments and criticisms of those who didn't like what he did. We are told in the Gospel that when Jesus cast out devils rather than accepting the power of God to deal with evil some of the people began a whispering campaign against Jesus. They even accused him of casting out evil through the power of evil, which is a ludicrous suggestion. Why would evil cast out evil? It is in fact the whispering and the judging and the pointing of the finger that comes from an evil source because it maims and destroys. The word Satan actually means the accuser. How did Jesus cope with that? By drawing upon the power of love that was within him and letting it be his answer. That only happens when we have faced love and allowed love to begin to transform us. Metanoia once again.

Much of the journey into metanoia is about focusing on what it is within us that makes us divide and separate and point the finger at others. It's a time for decision when we choose that the way of separation and blame is not the way that we will follow. As those who follow Jesus we have to decide whether we will walk his way of acceptance healing forgiveness trusting that this will lead us to life. Metanoia is the only way to move from our paranoid defensive patterns of thought that most of us are trapped in.

I recently met someone who was very badly damaged as a child. Her father died. Her mother killed herself because of the pain of loss. This woman ended up being raised by her grandmother who seemed unable to show any love at all. She was beaten regularly whether she had done something wrong or not. Her grandmother died and she went to live with some cousins and there she was abused. As a result of all of this her whole way of thinking has been defensive. She attacks before she is attacked. She is suspicious and refuses to trust anyone. She is unwilling to let go and never wants to be taken for a fool. She has never been able to see the good in anything. Indeed she presumes badness rather than goodness. Life is tainted by what happened to her and yet she is aware of the Gospel call to turn around and face the light, to let love overwhelm her. That is the movement from paranoia to metanoia that brings life.

CHAPTER THREE

EVERY DAY GOD

For most of my early life I remember knowing a wonderful lady called Winnie. She had a really hard life. She was born in 1903. At the age of seven her mother and father were killed in a freak accident when a carriage overturned and crushed them to death. She was put into an orphanage run by nuns where she spent her schooldays. It was a tough regime for a little girl to be exposed to. Winnie wasn't the sharpest knife in the drawer so when the time came for Winnie to leave school it was deemed that she should work in a hotel. At the age of fourteen she became the kitchen maid in a large hotel in Southport. She remained there for several years and eventually was trained as a cook, although never the chef! She worked in hotels in Southport and Liverpool and then she saw an advert in a magazine advertising for a companion to an elderly lady. Throwing caution to the winds she answered the advert and got the job. She soon discovered that the job was not all that it was cut out to be. There was an old lady who was bed bound, living in a huge house but there was no other domestic help apart from Winnie. She cleaned floors on corridors that went on for ever. She seemed to spend all her days if she wasn't cleaning, cooking, and answering the old lady's bell. There was certainly no companionship between the two of them. Her faith was the only security she had. She was a simple woman who loved God and loved people.

I met her when I was eleven and she was sixty nine. After the elderly lady died, Winnie had gone back to hotel work. Then the war had broken out and she was a cook in the army. She spent several years after the war working and living in other people's houses as a paid servant. I'm not sure how it happened but she eventually met Mrs Boyle a wealthy widow who was about ten years older than Winnie. They became firm friends and eventually moved into a house together. Winnie received a small wage as Mrs Boyle's companion and even though they were friends there was a clear line between the two of them. Mrs Boyle remained Mrs Boyle and Winnie was always Winnie My mum met the two of them when she was part of the ladies of Charity and became very friendly with Mrs Boyle.

Whenever Mrs Boyle came to our house Winnie would come too and they both quickly became part of our extended family. For nearly forty years I had birthday cards and Christmas cards and presents that Winnie knitted by hand. I remember her knitting a coat for our dog Sally who had never worn a coat in her life. What self respecting dog living in Liverpool would! The coat was bright red with yellow flashes running across it. It fitted where it touched. Winnie thought it looked wonderful. When my brother Paul came in he took one look at the dog and collapsed with laughter, tears streaming down his face. Sally stood up walked past him and went and stood in my mum and dad's wardrobe until the coat was removed and her dignity restored. Everything Winnie and Mrs Boyle did was done with a heart full of love that I probably never really appreciated at the time.

Eventually Mrs Boyle died and Winnie was left in the house by herself but without the Mrs Boyle she found life very hard. She had hardly any money to live on and life was tough. Still she never complained and whenever I visited her it was the same smiling face and warm hug that greeted me. She lived for about ten years more. In the Liverpool echo after she died there was just one notice from people she worked with in a Charity shop and it said this 'to a lovely lady who radiated love to all she met.' Winnie had nothing in the eyes of the world, no power, no wealth, and a life of hardship and yet in many senses she had everything because she loved and her love proclaimed the Kingdom of God. I learnt so much from her about simplicity and gratitude and love. I learnt that even in difficult circumstances life could be lived and enjoyed and that everything was a gift given with love. The gift of metanoia.

That encounter and other experiences that I have had have made me realise just how the whole process of conversion and transformation works. Primarily God uses the circumstances of our lives to change us and lead us more deeply into the truth of love if we only have eyes to see. I have been, and am being, converted through my experiences as a child, through my journey into seminary and Priesthood, through all the experiences I have had since then, good and bad, and through the people I have met. Nothing is wasted in the process of life. Everything belongs and all of it, the muddy twisted path that we call life, is leading us into the mystery of God.

The Gospels were written years after the death of Jesus. What had happened to those communities during those years was that they recognised in their midst the presence of Jesus. He was acting within their community not in some vague spiritual sense but in the community of believers. He was with them in so far as they were willing to love one another, forgive one another, not judge or condemn one another. He was with them in so far as they were able to be peace makers and healers. In some senses we have lost that awareness of the risen Jesus in our midst touching and sanctifying humanity. We would rather look outside ourselves at what we call holy things than within to discover the risen Lord. We would rather travel to places of pilgrimage to find Jesus than to look at our brother or sister or the circumstances of our lives. I love the story in the Acts of the Apostles when the disciples stand looking into the sky after the risen Jesus has ascended and an angel appears and says to them, 'What are you doing looking into the sky. Jesus has gone before you into Galilee.' You will find this Lord in the substance of your life and life will change you. Life will bring metanoia if you let it.

I have often wondered why we spend so much time looking outside of the ordinary for the Lord and I guess it is because to find Jesus in the midst of the community is not an easy task. It calls for faithfulness to those around us when we least want to be faithful. It calls for a willing-ness to believe in the goodness of another person. It demands that at times we have to be weak and vulnerable and willing to trust. It is a difficult road to travel but it is what spirituality is about. Anything that divorces us from the human and stops us finding the God who is in our midst is not a real spirituality. Look into your lives and dis-cover God. Reflect on every encounter that you have and you will see the face of Christ and know his presence with you always yes to the end of time and it will transform you.

18-12-14

Just before I was born my mum, dad, gran, and my brother moved house from a small terrace to a brand new flat on a recently-built council estate. Three other families moved

at the same time and the women of those families and my
mum hit it off and became firm friends in a friendship
that lasted for many years. Even after they had all left
the flats and gone their separate ways they remained in
contact and down the years there were frequent meetings
and visits to one another's houses. One of them, Marie,
had a daughter Rosalind who has severe learning and
physical difficulties. She is four years older than me and
communication was always difficult. Rosalind loved
jewellery and when she came to our house she would raid
my mum's box and all the cheap costume jewellery would
come out and Rosalind would sit on the stairs rocking back
and forth playing with the beads and the necklaces. She
was never excluded from anything. Wherever Marie and
her family went Rosalind went too. I think Rosalind has
taught me never to be frightened of difference. She has
taught me to accept and include those who might be
excluded. She has helped me to realise that patience
understanding and compassion for anyone are always
right. Even though I was unaware metanoia was happening
within me.

Paula D'Arcy says that 'God comes to us disguised as our
lives.' If you look at the resurrection appearances in Mark
and Matthew you find the women being told to go to
the apostles and tell them that Jesus is risen and has
gone before them to Galilee. Galilee is a symbol of the

ordinariness of life. If you read John's Gospel you find that after all the events of Holy week the disciples go back to what they are sure of. They go fishing and it is there they discover Jesus and have breakfast with him. God comes to us disguised as our lives. It is in the nitty gritty of our ordinary lives that God's outrageous grace is working. It is there that the spark of the divine is discovered and will work.

That is primarily where metanoia takes place, not necessarily in our religious gatherings or our prayer times, but in the struggle to believe or the hardness of heart that we are confronted with. As we journey, discovering what it means to be fully human we will meet Jesus. We will meet him in our emotions, in our experiences, but we have to start walking. We have to start trusting and believing that he is on the road of life and that just as he once was at work in Galilee, he is still at work today in the hearts and mind of those who are willing to look for him in the world.

We can find the God of Jesus in the ordinary stuff of humanity. Metanoia can happen in and through the mundane mess of our existence. Sadly we want the policeman God or the magical God who is a bit like the Father Christmas in the sky or the magician who does tricks. We would do anything rather than believe in the God who is present in the ordinariness of life and who, because of that presence, transforms the ordinariness.

A well known spiritual director and writer described his meeting with a hermit on a path in a wood. He was spending a year in a hermitage and he met this man whose whole life was lived in solitude. My friend decided not to speak to him but to respect his space and so went to pass him and the hermit stopped him and said ' when you go back tell the people you meet that God is not out there.' In the ordinariness of our stories and of our reactions to them is the presence of God.

Metanoia happens in the good and bad times of our lives. My brother Paul died recently and it has been one of the most difficult times of my life. Paul and I had become very close in recent years and shared an awful lot. He was my big brother and I loved him. There were just the two of us so he was the only other person who really knew our story and our struggle as children. He was a larger than life character who had forged a life in the Philippines that he loved with a wife and a daughter who meant everything to him. When he was diagnosed with cancer he faced it with his usual bullish attitude. Nothing would defeat Paul Thomas but sadly it did and when he died I was bereft and the sadness of his not being there remains with me and at times overwhelms me. It was a metanoia time when I was being invited again in the midst of pain to face love and let love free me and heal me. I was being asked to go deeper and trust and believe that God was enough.

Jesus enabled people to touch the divine in the material. So how do we become aware of that truth? A friend of mine at the end of every day examines her consciousness and asks questions like where have I been aware of the presence of God today? Where have I sensed God's presence? What has moved me or changed me today? Where was I emotionally touched without quite knowing why?

Open your eyes and see the God who is everywhere. Know that, as H. G. Wells said, 'Each moment of life is a miracle and mystery.' Metanoia is a process that we are invited into. It goes on for the whole of our lives as we are led more deeply into the mystery of God. It has little to do with sin and repentance in the narrow way we have understood that word. It has everything to do with turning to face the power of love and letting love lead you where love chooses to lead.

CHAPTER FOUR

POWER AND CONTROL

A few years ago I was at meeting down in the Cotswolds and while I was there I went into the chapel to pray and my eyes were drawn to the cross on the wall. It was a roughly hewn cross but it was the figure on it that drew my attention. The figure was the gauntest most twisted broken Christ I had ever seen. I sat there looking at it for ages just trying to let it speak to me.

Some hours later I was talking to someone and I asked them about the cross and was told that it had been carved by a young man in the throes of depression. He had tried to commit suicide several times and it was at his most broken and most weak that he had carved that figure. It was his own weakness and brokenness that hung there.

We spend so much energy avoiding our brokenness, avoiding failure, avoiding questioning the legitimacy of the systems we live by when in fact we need to enter into that sort of questioning for metanoia to happen. It is almost as though God says give me your failure and I will bring life out of it. Give me your lives with their brokenness pain confusion and pettiness and the death you experience will give way to abiding life. That is the example Jesus gives, hanging on the cross. Everything can be transformed. God can draw life from anything. This is our hope as followers of Jesus and it is the hope of the world now and forever. Metanoia has to happen within us for the plan of God to be fulfilled.

Many years ago I took part in a seminar on team building. As part of the exercise we watched an episode of Dallas in which J. R. was moving in on a take over bid. As we watched it we were asked to note the ways in which J. R. handled the bid and then to compare it with ourselves, with the world and with the Church. It was a real wake up call for those of us who thought we had moved beyond the power needs of the world. We began to recognise that we were as much caught up with the need for power as everybody else we just expressed that need in different ways. We needed metanoia as much as everyone else

Psychologists tell us that one of the main drives within the human psyche is for power. As individuals all of us at the seminar seemed to need power and control over others. We realised that the results of that need could be very damaging for the people around us. As nations our need to control other nations leads to catastrophic results. As a Church, burdened by the malaise of clericalism, we seem to be far more into power structures than the empowering of people. I think it would be fair to say that with the advent of Pope Francis it seems to be beginning to change, thank goodness. If it is to be more than a superficial change, if it is to involve the heart and the guts the Spirit has to be at work

Power and manipulation are never the way of Jesus. In Matthew's Gospel, James and John obviously completely misunderstood the Lord. Indeed we are told in each of the synoptic Gospels that the disciples were intoxicated with power. The disciples needed metanoia, to turn away from the systems that gave them security and look to the light. It did not take Jesus long to tell them that the Kingdom is not about power but about simple trusting relationship in which we grow and fulfil our potential. For those who follow Jesus power over others is never the way. We are to be people who love and serve. We are to be open and inclusive and encourage people to share their giftedness.

At another point in Luke's Gospel the disciples are arguing about power and who is the greatest and Jesus takes a little child to show them what a Kingdom person is like. In Jewish terms a child was outside the world of production, outside the power systems and in the eyes of society useless. Children were nothing that mattered. Children were simply not adults and all that pulls us into. It was a very radical concept for them and it is for us too, because it means a letting go of the games that we play with one another. It means a letting go of the power that we think we have and that is true of the Church as well and becoming in the world's eyes useless.

What are the Gospels saying to us? I think it's this, that if we want to experience the kingdom we have to become like little children. We have to let go of our blindness which is caused by the pain and hurt that many of us go through. We have to let go of the walls of cynicism and bitterness that we build up to protect ourselves. It is an invitation to turn around and begin to see the world and people through five year old eyes, unclouded, full of joy at the experience of being alive, full of joy in the God who gives life. *20 - 12 - 14*

It is an invitation to be present. Enter into that most simple level of presence without any need for power, without any need for status, or control. Once you become capable of presence at the simplest level, like the presence of a child, then you will become capable of true presence at every level. You become capable of presence to God and to your brothers and sisters. Learn how to be present, how to give and receive love and then you will experience the kingdom of God.

As Church, we should show an alternative to the world's power system showing that fullness of life does not depend on controlling people or situations but on following the Jesus way of loving service. This involves letting go of our own need for power and control. So we need the Spirit the only power that can transform us within and by which that process of letting go takes place.

The clarion call to metanoia comes from the mouth of John the Baptist who makes his entrance at the beginning of each of the synoptic Gospels. I doubt that John if he appeared today would make it into any university or already existing Church with his ranting and raving. People would not have anything to do with him. We have become very proper and staid. Anyone who tells us to reform, to change, and to turn back to our roots we do not really want to know. Basically that is what John is doing.

I was once invited to give a talk about change at a conference. Afterwards a woman came up to me and said something like, 'But God loves us as we are, and if we can't change, that's all right isn't it?' When she said it, I remembered the words of Megan McKenna who is a fiery American theologian and has much to challenge the Church with. She was at a conference on Spirituality called 'Come and See' that I help to organise. She invited people to reflect on change. During the session people broke into small groups and afterwards Megan took some feedback. One man said to her 'change is really hard and after all we're only human.'

Megan towered over this man and said in a voice that brooked no argument, 'You are not only human you have the spark of the divine within you, the power to do whatever you choose to do'. Probably a little more gently I said the same to this woman. She went away looking very sad because I think in fact she did not really want to change. I was very depressed some years ago and had to have a lot of therapy to help me get a hold on life again. My therapist at the time who is a very wise woman said to me there are no such words as can not only will not.

The common misunderstanding that many Christians make is to think that all Jesus preached about was love. I really think that is a misrepresentation. I don't think that Jesus came just to preach about loving. He came to preach change and transformation or metanoia. It is because of that change that love is possible. Jesus didn't give that many teachings on how to love but he does constantly teach about change and faces us with stories that shake the very foundation of who we are if we listen to them. I think it is essential in understanding the gospel at more than just a cerebral level that we recognise that Jesus is a preacher about repentance or change following in the line of John the Baptist. That is why John the Baptist is always put in the Gospels as preceding Jesus, because he is a great preacher of change.

So let us look at the teaching of John the Baptist. The Dead Sea Scrolls are a collection of 981 texts discovered between 1946 and 1956 at Khirbet Qumran in the West Bank in Israel. They were found inside caves about a mile inland from the northwest shore of the Dead Sea. From all that has been discovered it seems as though a sect had broken apart from main line Judaism and very much returned to tradition of Israel. These scrolls were discovered near where this community lived in the desert and they seemed to detail the rule of life for the community.

One of the constant rituals undertaken by the community was that of purification which you will find detailed in Leviticus Ch 11-15. Tertullian was a prolific early Christian author from Carthage in the Roman province of Africa. He was probably the first Christian author to produce a lot of Latin Christian literature. He wrote this about the purification rituals of the Jews. 'The Jew washes himself every day because every day he is defiled.' Symbolic washing and purifying was woven into the very fabric of Jewish ritual. In many religions those purification rites have become a symbol of washing away of the past and the beginning of a new life. To be baptised a means to be plunged into something and it probably came out of the Qumran tradition.

The Baptist came out of the desert maybe from that community or one similar. Using his own experience he takes the symbol of a ritual bath and makes it into a symbol for people who are ready to change. The important matter to reflect on is the conversion, the repentance, and the change of heart. We are to be turned around so that we become a new creation.

When we believe that God loves us then we enjoy the forgiveness of sins. We do not have to earn forgiveness, just look to the light. God is ready to give love totally at any moment. As soon as we are ready to receive it and believe it and enjoy it we will. We tend to substitute anything for that truth, money, sex, power. It is the way of the world and only changing from it will open us to love that transforms and leads us into fullness of life. John the Baptist has to live such a radical lifestyle to tell us not sell out to this world. He is telling us that we have got to live for the Kingdom of God to find life.

Metanoia is not always terribly visible. It is something that happens deep within. When you are living your ordinary life and you realise that the way in which you are living is inadequate and empty. It happens when the systems that make sense of life are suddenly up for grabs and you are looking for the more. Some writers say that it is then that you are intuitively in the Kingdom of God and metanoia is beginning to happen. So are you prepared to turn around and let go of the need for power and control? Are you prepared to face love and in the facing be transformed deeply? If you are, carry on reading; who knows where it might lead you?

CHAPTER FIVE

THE KINGDOM

A few months ago I found myself in a retreat centre in Yorkshire. There was to be a week spent in silence reflecting on Luke's Gospel and I had been asked to provide the input. At the end of each session I always asked those who had gathered to share anything that had struck them. One of the sisters who was part of the group told us a story of the day that she was travelling on a bus between Bombay and Calcutta. The bus pulled into a compound to drop people off and so that the driver could have a break. The sister said that she got off the bus and went and sat in the cool of a doorway to eat her lunch. The compound was run by the Missionaries of Charity. After a while a door opened and a young boy came out beaming and holding in his hand a small bag of sugar. He told sister that he had been very ill but against all the odds he had recovered and today he was going home. The bag of sugar which is a very precious commodity in India had been given him by the sisters who were so delighted at his recovery.

While they were talking a group of people entered the compound carrying a small child on a stretcher. He had malaria.

The sister who was telling us the story began to cry as she told how the little boy rushed over to the stretcher and gave the sick child his gift of sugar. It was such a powerful moment for her and for us. Here was this child probably dying being given a gift that meant so much by another child. It was for me a real image of who God is and it challenged me yet again to realise that God is at home with dirt and mess. God is in the midst of brokenness and vulnerability. God is there in the darkness of sin and the pain of life.

So many of us think that we have to be perfect before we come to God, that God won't love us unless we've got the 'I's' dotted and the 'Ts' crossed. So many of us have an image of God where God is like some sort of moral custodian frowning on the messes we make and delighting when we get it wrong. Within all of us there is a temptation to wear the masks and play the games and be respectable so that somehow we can be acceptable. You don't have to be acceptable to be in the Kingdom, you simply have to be open to love and compassion and mercy.

The Kingdom of God is never defined by the way in which we human beings like to define things. It is not about whether or not we live good moral lives or whether we belong to a Church and fulfil the law of that Church. In the Kingdom there are all sorts of people. Matthew says to us that the kingdom is like a dragnet cast into the sea that brings in a haul of all kinds. It is not just the perfect who are there but all those who are open. It reminds me that God works in messy situations. God is at peace with lives that are falling apart and with emotions and feelings that are ragged and painful. God won't be bound by our pathetic attempts to be respectable and acceptable and won't work in the ways we expect God to. God is comfortable with mess and difference.

It seems to me that the invitation to live in the Kingdom is three-fold. Firstly that we should never tie God down and presume that we know who God is and how God works. It is an invitation always to be open to love, compassion and mercy and to know that wherever we see them, God is at work and that's not always in the tidy understandings of life that we've given ourselves.

Secondly it is an invitation to be real about ourselves and to admit the mess and brokenness and pain and vulnerability and sin is within all of us and know that God is comfortable with that and wants to bring healing and peace and forgiveness. You don't have to be respectable with God. The kingdom is full of people who haven't got it together but who know what brings life.

Thirdly it challenges us to be in the midst of brokenness

and pain allowing the presence of Jesus to be real in the lives of those who in whatever way find themselves shunned or prejudiced against. As individuals and as church we cannot write off people who do not fit or who appear to be different. We cannot ignore those who are not whatever 'respectable' may be. They may be in the kingdom far more fully than we are. I think it was St Augustine who said that there are many inside the Church that God does not have and there are many outside the Church that God does have.

One of the most wonderful men I have ever met was a Hindu by birth. He was married to an alcoholic who over the years they were together led him a merry dance. She would often disappear for days on end. When she was at home he never quite knew what she would do or what state she would be in. She constantly threatened him with divorce and embarrassed him on many occasions by turning up drunk at important occasions. She spent his money, re-mortgaged his house and on one occasion tried to kill him.

Never once did I see him angry. Never once did I see him despair of his situation. Never once did he say anything about his wife. He carried on his life with great dignity and with a compassion towards her that I do not think I have ever witnessed anywhere else. I asked him once how he managed and he smiled and said, 'Only with the good God do I cope'.

It seems to me that when the Kingdom is sorted out at the end of time we will be very surprised at who is there and who is not. One of the staff at the seminary where I trained to be a Priest often used to say that he thought we would get a surprise whenever we get to whatever heaven is. Why? Well it might not necessarily be full of those we thought. The Kingdom is always bigger and wider and more inclusive than we can ever imagine and our role is never to judge others but simply to be open to the reality of the kingdom which is full of messed up people who try to love.

This kingdom is first of all a relationship, a relationship with the father who is the centre of all that is, which means it is a quality of relationship to everything else as well. To live in that relationship with the constant change that it demands is to enter into the process of metanoia.

The real questions to ask ourselves are have I entered into the experience? Have I turned round and let God make me a new creation? It is all about entering into a new relationship and letting the Spirit turn us inside out.

To be in the kingdom of God is a way of being and living

in the world, living in the here and now, rooted in life but with values that last eternally. That relationship between the 'now' and 'forever' is always in tension in the gospels It is never something we can totally realise.

We pray in the 'Our Father' for the coming of the kingdom. In a sense we always want more of it. Always wanting more is part of the 'not yet' character of the kingdom. We can never say 'we've got it or that we possess it'. Yet what the gospels want to assure us is that the kingdom of God is here, that there is enough of the kingdom for us to recognise it.

The only reason we can long for anything is because we have already experienced something of it. We can only really want something if we have had enough of it to know it is good, so the gospel proclamation wants to encourage us that the kingdom is here. *23 = 12 = 14*

As I have already mentioned, I am not a Greek scholar but I have been told that there are four Greek words which are foundational in understanding what the Gospel and the Kingdom is all about. These words are metanoia, basiliea, agape and therapeia. The word metanoia is at the heart of this book and I hope you have gained something of a flavour of what it means. Basiliea means the kingdom. Agape is translated as the law of love and therapeia the whole dynamic of healing.

The core of Jesus' understanding is that you change radically, not just adopting that old chestnut of saying sorry for your sins. As you change you begin to adopt a completely alternative point of view to the prevailing world view. You begin to live in a different reality where heaven and earth are no longer separate. This change in understanding leads you to a life based on love where you have a deep and counter cultural love for others, particularly the poor and the broken where you become a healer.

To really live in the Kingdom comes at a cost. It invites you to give up an understanding of life that might have been your only way of understanding. You are invited to live by a set of values that do not reward the ego. Sadly, much of what we do is egocentric, even the religious things, even the spiritual things. We do them because they make us feel good.

Kingdom living will face you with the challenge of undertaking values that contradict the lifestyle of those around you. To live in the Kingdom demands courage but 'be brave', said Jesus, 'for I have conquered the world.' Metanoia pulls us towards the Kingdom of God and it is then the work of the spirit to lead us more deeply into metanoia. The sense of sadness I have is that after that, after sensing metanoia happening within, many just become more religious rather than radically different.

That radical change is all about seeing and knowing the Kingdom in our midst. It reveals the truth that God is everywhere and in everything. To believe that God is in everything means that we can no longer divide and separate and say who is in the kingdom or who is outside it. It means we have to learn to live with difference. It means we have to choose to find goodness in all things. It means we have to learn to respect the created order. It means that we have to hold the tension refusing to judge or condemn even when that's demanded of us. God is everywhere and in everything. Radical metanoia opens up that truth for us. That change of heart and mindset is hugely challenging if we really take it seriously.

For centuries the Church believed that there was no salvation outside its walls. God was only at work in the lives of those who professed certain truths. Pope Francis has recently said 'I have a dogmatic certainty: God is in every person's life. God is in everyone's life. Even if the life of a person has been a disaster, even if it is destroyed by vices, drugs or anything else - God is in this person's life. You can - you must - try to seek God in every human life.' God is everywhere and salvation happens in the most unlikely of places.

The issue is only how open are you to God and how willing are you to search for truth and to change because of your search. To experience the Kingdom depends on how full of compassion and love you are becoming. God is bigger than our understanding. God is bigger than the Church's understanding. God is always more and any attempts we make to put God in a box, any efforts we make to limit who God is and how God works means we are just playing at discovering the richness of God.

In Luke's Gospel Jesus stood up in the temple at Nazareth and proclaimed the Lord's year of favour to all people, the Good news to the poor and the broken and everyone thought he was wonderful until he started to put it into practice and did not distinguish between Jew and Gentile. He lived a life where status held no sway and those who were outside the temple system were suddenly within the heart of God.

We can be exactly the same, happy to embrace the Gospel until it pushes our narrow provincial hearts and minds, until we are pushed to be compassionate and loving and accepting of all people, until we are invited to expand our hearts and minds and see goodness everywhere.

If we were to read the rest of that passage from Luke's Gospel we would see how Jesus challenged the Jews to be open to the presence of God in others. The Jews of Jesus time hated the Sidonians because they were not Jewish.

The Jews also hated the Syrians because they were not Jewish. The presumption was that God too hated the Sidonians and the Syrians. What happens is that Jesus, who after all was only the son of the Carpenter, tells them that God was at work in the lives of a Sidonian widow and a Syrian leper. Jesus was challenging them to let go of their image of God and recognise the truth that God is always more than we can imagine. That is what the Kingdom is all about.

You see, as soon as we allow ourselves to believe that God is on our side and not on the side of others, we can allow ourselves the luxury of prejudice. In its worst forms this gives rise to horrors like the Holocaust or ethnic cleansing, all because of some differential we care to put on people. Jesus is reminding us that if we say that we are open to God there is no room for any sort of bias because God is present in all things and is working through all things.

So whatever there is within you that would make you look at another person or group of people and say God is not there and cannot be at work, remember the synagogue at Nazareth and face your prejudices and judgemental attitudes so that you will see the glory of God at work all over the world. To live in and experience the Kingdom we have to be willing to allow metanoia to happen within us, and it turns us upside down. I often wonder how much we really want to live in the Kingdom with all that it brings?

CHAPTER SIX

WHEN THE SPIRIT COMES

A few years ago I was at home trying to make sense of a document that my brother had left me to look at. Paul was my big brother who died in 2013. He always asked me questions about the papers that he gave me to look at. Most of the time I failed to understand them and in the end gave up reading them, so I usually looked pretty stupid when he asked those questions . It was very obvious to him that I had not read them so this on this particular occasion I decided I would spend some time looking at something Paul had left me, just to show him that I was not completely thick. Oh, the best laid plans of mice and men!

In the background I had the television on and it was the 'Pride of Britain awards' that was showing. The document soon went on one side as I was caught up in the stories that were being told. I love stories. I found myself terribly moved, particularly by Tariq Jahan the man whose son had been killed during the riots that England experienced in 2011. Whatever he may or may not have done since, I watched this man who had immense dignity in the midst of his sorrow talking about compassion and love and peace. As has often happened to me, in him I saw the face of God. I saw God who is torn apart by the pain of the world but motivated by love that knows no end and the desire for peace in the hearts of all men and women.

That challenges the image of God that so many of us seem to have. For many people their image of God is a remote authoritarian figure whose love is conditional and dependent on us being good. Even for those of us who have begun to see that God is more there is often a lingering doubt about love and compassion, usually because it challenges our own need for revenge and to make people pay for what they do. I get more hassle when I preach about God's love than I do when I preach about anything else.

When Jesus teaches his disciples to pray he asks them to imagine a God whose love and compassion is more than anything in their experience. What the Gospels seem to be saying is that God is more than we can ever imagine, but more than that there is nothing to fear from a God whose only desire is to love and to respond to our deepest need.

The image of God that was around at the time of Jesus was of a petty small minded God, a God that people lived in fear of. It was that image of a God who had to be appeased and obeyed that many of the Old Testament prophets tried so hard to break.

One of the most beautiful insights of the prophets was into the faithfulness of God. Hosea who was writing about 800 BC communicated this in a very special way as he took back his unfaithful wife Gomer in response to what the Lord asked of him. She ran away again and Hosea took her back and then again. It led Hosea to recognise what Israel had done to God. God's love kept reaching out to Israel, constantly drawing her back always wanting to start afresh. God was faithful even though the people weren't. Hosea was to do what God was doing so the people could see what God was like.

Jeremiah saw failure and despair throughout his prophetic ministry. He was faithful to his call to be a prophet and yet had seen no response. Finally he realised that human beings will never respond freely to God and so, Jeremiah falls back on the initiative of God. God is going to do it. The new covenant that he and Ezekiel become aware of is totally at God's initiative. It is not dependant on our repentance, worthiness or goodness. When are we going to believe it? God says 'then I will be their God and they shall be my people'. As the prophets come to experience God's unconditional love, they are able to respond to God, but it is only because they have first experienced

God pouring love out on them. That experience of unconditional love becomes the reality of the new covenant and from that comes the new people that God is creating.

Isaiah says to the people of his day, and to us, that our religious practice is empty unless it's leading us into relationship with a God who can only love you. When you know that to be true, you will know that you can always hope in God whatever may be going in your life. You will know that God is coming to save you despite the mess that is within you. You will trust and love because you have been trusted and loved. That will change the way you see the world, the way you see other people, the way you understand politics and economics and Religion. Isaiah saw that because of the love that is poured out upon us, we should be creating an alternative way of living.

Instead, we've become the place, certainly in Western Europe, where nice middle class people go, not a radical alternative lifestyle that has it's roots in a God who has lavished us with love. I often say to people that we are really not very different than the rest of the world. We are not bad, we just believe what everyone else believes but use religious language to express it.

I could keep on reflecting on the Prophets' experience. I

could keep on repeating their desire that God's people know the truth of who God is, but I hope you get the message clearly that they were challenging the people of Israel to open their hearts to metanoia.

If the Kingdom of God is primarily about a relationship with God and then about our relationship with the created order it seems to me that the first reality that metanoia has to challenge is our image of God. Amongst those who believe in God there is often a sense of limitation; 'Yes, God loves us, but...'

A few years ago I was speaking in Birmingham and as I usually do, I began to speak about the unconditional love of God. I never know where else to start. After the talk there was a queue of people waiting to speak to me all because they did not dare believe in the unconditional nature of God's love. Yes, there was a tacit belief in the love of God but almost to a person they were convinced that we had to do our bit.

About six years ago at the Celebrate Conference the main speaker was talking about God's love and as part of his presentation he showed a DVD that reduced the 1000 people in the audience to tears. The DVD was called Team Hoyt and it told the story of Dick and Rick Hoyt, a father-and-son team from Massachusetts. For the past 25 years or more Dick, who is now almost 70, has pushed and pulled his son across the country and over hundreds of finish lines. When Dick runs, Rick is in a wheelchair and Dick is pushing. When Dick cycles, Rick is in the seat attached to the front of the bike. When Dick swims, Rick is in a small boat being pulled by Dick.

At Rick's birth in 1962 the umbilical cord coiled around his neck and cut off oxygen to his brain. His parents were told that there would be no hope for their child's development. He eventually learned to communicate through an interactive computer and they learned then that Rick loved sports and really wanted to run marathons and triathlons and so his dad decided to fulfil his dream.

The reason it was so moving was because it spoke very powerfully of the love of God. The image of the Father responding to the needs of his son was a visual reminder of God's care for us. If God gave us life then surely we can trust God with our lives. We are loved beyond our wildest imaginings by God.

Richard Rohr in his book Great Themes of Scripture says,

> 'God's love is total, unconditional, absolute and forever. The state of grace - God's attitude toward us - is eternal. We are the ones who change. Sometimes we are able to believe that God loves us unconditionally,

absolutely and forever. That's grace! When we no longer believe God loves us, we can no longer love ourselves. We have to allow God to continually fill us. Then we find in our own lives the power to give love away.'

When we turn and face the love of God then change will happen within us. When we let go of our intransigence about doing our bit, transformation starts to happen. It has to, because that is the work of God; to share the reality of love which then has its own motivation to transform and free.

Whether we know it or not our deepest need is for the Spirit of God; the very life of God poured out for us so that we have the strength to live lives that are vibrant and full, to live as a person of hope, a person of justice, a person of love, compassion, and forgiveness, a person filled with awe and wonder who delights in every moment that is given.

When we allow God to release the Spirit within us then we begin to become aware that God is unconditionally loving. We come to realise that life is about entering into the most incredible encounter with the divine. The most incredible gift that God can give us is Godself and that gift is there for the asking. God will never withhold

Godself from us because God wants intimacy with us and wants us to share real life with us. That is why Luke says ask for the Spirit and the Spirit will be given search for the Spirit and you will find the Spirit knock and the door to life will be opened to you. The holy Spirit, the very energy of God, the power of God, the love of God given to us so that we would find the strength never to be defeated; given to us so that we can find the strength never to be overcome. The Holy Spirit is given to us that we might be for the world that sign of contradiction that in the midst of seeming disaster we can find the strength to be at peace and say, 'God is love'.

If only we could realise how much we are loved what freedom that would bring, freedom from anxiety and worry about what others think of us, the freedom to live in the present moment delighting in it without thinking or believing that we have to be anything other than the child we are. It would bring us freedom from ourselves as we learn to laugh at the foibles that make us who we are and it would give us the freedom to bring to God whatever we had to bring knowing that it would be met with love.

It would bring us the freedom of living in this world with the knowledge that we are living in something far bigger than ourselves which is eternal and which we are caught up in instead of being forever locked into the interminable question 'Am I going to heaven when I die?' You are already there, if you could but believe it. That's why Catherine of Siena could say that it is heaven all the way to heaven and hell all the way to hell.

It would bring us the freedom to love our brothers and sisters without an agenda, to accept and include rather than reject and exclude, to enter into dialogue with the world and to know that everything is gift from the one who is always the lover. I love the words from the children's book 'Wind in the Willows' when Mole and Rat have their encounter with the august presence and the author writes, 'He looked into the very eyes of the Friend and Helper.'

Love is the image of Godself that God wanted to plant in our hearts and when we encounter that love, when metanoia happens within us, then we will be on the road to freedom. It is almost too awesome to believe. Open your hearts to love and you will find freedom. That's when metanoia starts to happen.

CHAPTER SEVEN

MORE OF THE SPIRIT

I came across this quotation from Sai Baba a few months ago which has meant a great deal to me. 'Life is a song, sing it. Life is a game, play it. Life is a challenge, meet it. Life is a dream, realise it. Life is a sacrifice, offer it. Life is love, enjoy it.'

There is within that quotation a cry to really experience life to the full, to discover who we are and what life is about. The Gospel for me is primarily God's way of enabling me to understand what it means to be alive. Salvation is not about what happens to us in the future. It is not just about saving our souls. We are not just put on this earth to somehow endure it for the future grace-filled life that happens after we die. We are not just put here so that we can earn our way into heaven. God is the God of the present moment and wants us to live now.

The story of the wedding feast of Cana is all about the ordinariness of life being transformed into something alive and vibrant. The party runs out of wine and Mary the mother of Jesus says, 'They have no wine', stating the obvious... but

John wants us to know the deeper meaning. They have no joy, no life, no liberation. The cry is 'Set us free Lord.' Suddenly the Gospel has changed level and we are into the arena of the Spirit. Mary becomes a symbol of humanity crying out for new life. No longer 'Mother' but 'Woman'. What happens? Water is turned into wine. The best is still to come. We are to live lives to the full in the here and now, in the present moment. That is the work of the Spirit to enable us to live life to the full, to lead us into metanoia.

My Aunty Maureen loved life. She loved people, she loved God and despite the tragedies she had to go through she got the most out of life that she possibly could. She was intelligent, articulate, forthright, and at times stubborn and determined. She had a wicked sense of humour and was always interested in everything that was going on. Even when I'd only seen her twenty four hours earlier I had to dredge up some fresh news from somewhere. She talked to anyone and everyone, which was part of the reason why a shopping trip to Tesco's never took less than three hours. She was full of stories about her early life and about the Second World War. I used to think sometimes she had taken on Hitler single handed!

She loved going to the theatre and to concerts at the Philharmonic Hall. She loved her time working voluntarily in the galleries at the Bluecoat Chambers. She loved her garden and flowers and spring and summer but hated winter with a passion. She loved travel and was always encouraging people to go and experience other cultures and languages. She could never understand people who didn't take the opportunities if they could to go and see the world, particularly Europe.

She loved literature, poetry, and music. Much of her literature came back to her in her last days and she drove the carers mad reciting the lady of Shallot and other poems learnt by heart at school. We shared a passion for auctions and antiques and shared many outings to fairs, shops and auctions. I remember taking her out one day and as we got out of the car I spied a rocking chair I liked, so I said to aunty Maureen, 'You sit there on the bench while I have a quick look inside and then I'll come out'. By the time I did come out she had engaged the shop's owner in conversation and had done a deal on the rocking chair for herself.

Suffice to say, life did not pass aunty Maureen by. She grabbed hold of it with both hands and lived it. She even decided in latter years that sleeping was a waste of time. Not a minute was to be wasted. It was all too precious. At the heart of it all was faith, not a pious sentimental escapism but faith in a God who was with her and in whom she trusted. She often said to me that if God has given us life then who do we think we are we to waste it.

Before she died at the age of 93, I spent a great deal of time with my aunty Maureen. I used to take her shopping. It was always an adventure because of her feisty nature. I clearly remember taking her out one afternoon. When we came out of the shop I went to get the car leaving aunty Maureen leaning on the trolley. By the time I came back the wind had got up, the rain had begun to fall, and the trolley had gone hurtling off into the distance. Aunty Maureen was clinging to a pillar for dear life and laughing uproriously.

It struck me at the time that there is an incredible energy in wind, an incredible power. You only have to look at the devastation that hurricanes cause or the amount of power that's generated through those turbo-driven wind machines to recognise the energy.

The same is true of water. One of the most incredible experiences I have ever had was to sail into Niagara Falls on the Maid in the Mist. The noise was deafening. The force of the water was incredible. I was soaked within seconds despite the silly plastic macs the stewards on the boat give you to wear. I remember once standing at the foot of the Krimml falls in Austria which are the tallest falls Europe and watching the water cascading down and again filling me with a sense of power and energy and dynamism.

I also began to think about fire. When aunty Maureen and I returned from the shops I lit the fire and within seconds there was light and warmth filling the room. Like all of us, I have watched the news reports in past years of the fires in France and Australia where it was almost impossible to keep the fire under control. It could hardly be contained. Again there is an immense amount of power in fire, an immense amount of energy.

If you read the Gospels you find Jesus using all of those elements when he talks about the Spirit. In John's gospel you find him talking to Nicodemus about the wind that blows where it will. In Luke's Gospel you find him talking about baptising with fire. Again in John's Gospel you find John telling the story of the Samaritan woman and describing that she acted as though she had a fountain of living water bubbling up within her.

Why would Jesus use those elements to describe the Spirit? I guess it's because the Spirit is about energy and power and dynamism. It is so sad that we have reduced the action of the Spirit in our lives to a nominal pouring of water on our heads at Baptism or a quick slap on the cheek from the Bishop.

You might almost say that this Spirit is the energy of God given to us so that we can live our lives to the full. This is what Richard Rohr, the American Franciscan, says about the Spirit:

> 'The day of pentecost frees the apostles to believe in a God who is actively involved in their lives and no longer a mere intellectual belief. The Holy Spirit has become wind, fire, joy, excitement, universal shareability, and not just another boring sabbath obligation or more commandments to obey. Notice how all the metaphors of Spirit presence are dynamic, alive, moving, and universal.
>
> The Spirit will always be totally unmerited grace. She always takes the initiative. The Holy Spirit is experienced as intimacy and warmth and fire, as the power to love beyond boundaries and ethnicities. She is presented as surprising, elusive, and free, and yet totally given. The Spirit comes from no place we can control, least of all by our good behaviour or even our bad behaviour. All we can do is surrender and enjoy.'

30 -12

When we begin to realise that the Spirit is gift and is within us then we become witnesses to the reality of God. We are not necessarily witnesses because we are at Mass every day or we say our prayers. We are witnesses when we're alive deep within with an energy that challenges the grey existence that so many people think is life. We are witnesses when we live life as though every moment is gift and the world is wonderful. It is when we look at the world and everything in it with the eyes of a child and glimpse the glory of God everywhere. It is the Spirit who increases our capacity to live, but that will mean transformation and metanoia is needed.

We like to hold on to what's familiar and what makes sense of our lives, good things as well as bad. We hold on to patterns of life that we enjoy and we hold on to our bitterness and our anger because it's safe. The concept of metanoia threatens us and frightens us and we react to the possibility of it rather than respond to it. I have a sneaking suspicion that we're not supposed to be comfortable but open all the time to newness and difference if we're going to recognise God in all things.

I guess any Pentecost experience will change us within and clear our vision so that we can see that God is all around us, that the trinity of love is present in the very air we breathe. A sure fire way to discern how aware of the Spirit we are, how much of a Pentecost experience we've had, is to see how open we are to change and how vibrant our lives are.

Many years ago I was working with a young woman called

Michelle whose life was a mess. She'd got into the drug scene and was financing her habit by selling herself on the streets. At the same time she was desperately trying to get a degree, which seemed to be slipping from her grasp the further she fell into her spiral of self-destruction. She knew that only God could help her but her one big fear was opening herself to God because she was so frightened of changing within.

The Spirit is about change and transformation and I think that's why so many of us have such a problem with the Spirit. Like Michelle we can't cope with change and the call to inner transformation. If we are going to be really honest we don't like this part of God which we can't control or explain, this part of God which is fire and water and wind and which our theologies can't predict or inhibit.

If you look at the Gospel accounts of what happened after the resurrection, you read that the disciples were in an upper room frightened out of their lives, worried about what the Jews would do to them. Those same people in the Acts of the Apostles were filled with the power of the Holy Spirit; changed people who, rather than responding to their fears and their worries, became fearless proclaimers of the presence of the risen Jesus; people who could see the Lord everywhere.

That movement tells us something very important about the action of the Spirit that it is something that happens within us. The Pentecost story is not just some two thousand year old event that we pay lip service to but a living reality going on within us, working a miracle of transformation, moving us out of our ingrained attitudes and hardness of heart, turning us around to live a life that is vibrant, wild, and free.

The Spirit is the only reality that can set us free from our fears and our anxieties. How many of us are controlled by them? The Spirit is the only power with which we can face our inner poverty and brokenness with peace. We run away from it all the time rather than face it and own it. It is only through the presence of the Spirit that we can find the power to forgive and not judge and condemn. We spend so much energy holding on to things and pointing the finger at others. It is the only power that will help us deal with our self-righteousness and bigotry.

There's a sense in which we have to let go of what we thought faith was about and allow God to teach us what faith is really about. There is a very real sense in which we have to constantly immerse ourselves in the God who is creator, redeemer, and enlivener, so that God can reveal Godself to us again and again. If we do that it means that we have to let go of the way we see people and the world because if God is constantly revealing Godself to us it will mean that we see everything with new eyes. It is a scary place to be because it means a lot of our certainties and securities have to be let go as we wait and see what God will do.

If you are open to the Holy Spirit then the very stuff of your life will lead you into metanoia. The invitation that we are given is to open our hearts and say, 'Come Holy Spirit', and go on that journey which will lead us to life. A journey that is scary and challenging because it forces us to constantly let go and reassess what makes sense of life and what values are important in life. Don't say you believe in Pentecost if you don't want to change. Don't say you believe in Pentecost if there is no room in your life for becoming different. Let the Holy Spirit lead you into life where you see God everywhere and in everything.

The Spirit is at work in the Church and in the world wherever people are seeing with fresh eyes, wherever people are changing within and living lives of compassion and love and forgiveness and community. The Spirit is at work when the very stuff of our lives speaks to us of an ever-present God. The Spirit is at work in every act of kindness and love.

The Spirit has been given to lead us into a deep place of

radical conversion where we know in the depths of our guts that God is present in even the very air that we breathe and where every moment is gift. We need metanoia so that we begin to see completely differently than we might have done otherwise and realise the truth of presence. It is so that we can look at every human person and know that, whether they be Hindu, Moslem Buddhist, or Christian, they are a child of God. It is so that we can see beyond the chaos and the mess and the violence and know that the world is gift and God is present with us in it. It brings an end to judgement and condemnation. It opens us up to otherness. It lessens fear and it allows us to be open and searching all the time for more of God.

The Spirit we have been given is about real things. It is about being open to newness in everything. So pray every day for the courage to allow the Spirit to immerse us in power so that we can change within and live in the world of change with faith and hope.

CHAPTER EIGHT

SIGN OF CONTRADICTION

A few of months ago I was in London for a meeting but had time while I was there to go and see the J.B. Priestley play 'An Inspector Calls'. It's a fascinating insight into the way power and wealth corrupts and the ways in which we will do anything to protect what we value and usually the things that are of significance to us are illusory and passing. It challenged me to ask myself the question, 'What do I hold on to and try and protect at the expense of the things that are real'?

The next day I went to the meeting and listened to the story of a community in Korea made up of people who society rejects who have nothing in the eyes of the world, no power, no wealth. Many have both physical and learning difficulties and yet these people have together provided a place of love support healing and life. Together they stand as a real beacon to the love that proclaims the Kingdom of God and I heard again in my heart the prayer that emerged the first weekend that I spent with Sr Helen Prejean, the nun whose work with those on death row is both challenging and inspiring. Deep within myself I found myself praying, 'Lord make it as real in me as it is in her'.

I was challenged not to escape into a false piety where all I do is serve myself and my own needs. Let my prayer take me to a place of real loving service that is the Kingdom. Of course I know that metanoia is key to that prayer becoming reality and is a constant process calling me deeper and deeper into the mystery that is God.

As I look around the world I am convinced that people are desperate to hear the real Gospel. There are in every country across the world people who are desperate for love that is not conditional and does not depend on who they are or what they are like. You and I are sent out to preach the Kingdom of God. We are to love. It is to be real love, not conditioned by our petty moralising about who is deserving and who is not. Our primary purpose is to be people of love, forgiveness, and reconciliation. Without metanoia, that deep radical change within, our love will never be Gospel love but will always be tainted by self interest and self preservation.

If we are invested in this world, and caught up in the need for materialism and power that seem to make this world tick then it is very difficult to be a witness to the gospel. It is so sad that the church seems to present to the world an image of wealth and power and security. In many ways it can appear as though we have sold out and we are not living for the kingdom of God. It's so sad that we need our status symbols: 'I am a Eucharistic minister.' 'I am a catechist.' 'I am a reader.' 'I am a priest' (or a sister); as though any of those things matter.

All that is important is that we proclaim the kingdom of love. What does that mean in a practical sense? It means that we have to question our attitudes towards the refugee and the asylum seeker, towards the single mothers and those on benefits. It means that we can not be hard-hearted towards the little ones in society or towards those who do not fit the norm. To be Christian is to be someone who loves and who proclaims love to every person and in every situation. We have to challenge the world's view by loving those whom the world finds unacceptable.

If you go back into the Scriptures you will find this call to be radically different right at the core of the ancient books. I would like to concentrate on the book of the prophet Isaiah because he or she along with Amos and probably Ezekiel has a clear call to metanoia and therefore becoming a sign of contradiction for the world.

During Isaiah's time there were a lot of alliances with other nations - Egypt, or Syria, or Assyria. Each time the people are tempted to enter into such an alliance the prophet says,

'No, trust in God'. Isaiah is amazingly politically involved, which makes me smile at those who say the church should not be involved in politics. Isaiah speaks into the contemporary situation. He assesses the political situation and has something to say and the people he is speaking to, if you read chapter 1:2, don't like it. It is always the way.

One of the themes that develops within Isaiah's writing is that of the remnant or the few who really hear. Once the prophet starts talking about politics then the vast majority of the religious people are not interested any more. When it was just about offering sacrifice and worshipping God it was acceptable because it did not really impinge on their lifestyle. Isaiah begins to speak about lack of integrity and truth and Israel is starting to become a remnant. Metanoia will always take us to difficult places. The remnant has got to learn to accept that the word they preach is never going to be accepted by everyone. When the gospel is really preached numbers go down, especially when it demands commitment.

When I was appointed as a Parish Priest I was extremely anxious. I was recovering from a period of depression and I wanted to be liked and accepted. The first Saturday night I went out to a packed Church and celebrated Mass and preached with my usual blend of story and Gospel values. Mass took about fifty minutes. That night I got my first abusive phone call from someone who had not liked what I had said and who expected Mass to be over in half an hour. I had a couple of anonymous letters and several irate phone calls during the week which affected me badly. By the time I came out of the sacristy the following Saturday I was a neurotic mess just about in control of myself. The congregation had halved in numbers and at communion time there was a mass exodus so that we were left with barely one hundred people at the end of Mass. When I saw my spiritual director later in the week his response was to laugh and say 'it was ever thus.' If you preach the Gospel you will always upset people who don't want metanoia.

Isaiah tries to shock people so that they can hear what he is saying. There is nothing wrong in having our comfort zones punctured occasionally. It is one way in which we can grow providing we ask the right questions and are open to change. That is one of the things that metanoia does. Isaiah goes on to condemn all the religious practices of the day. In our terms it would be all the processions, Friday devotions, and novenas. It's almost as though God is saying 'I hate them with all my soul. The games you create to win my love don't mean a thing.' 2 - 2 - 14

What Isaiah is inviting us to reflect on is this: if there were deep integrity within us then we would live in love and harmony with concern for our brother or sister at the centre of everything. This would affect us personally, nationally, globally. Isaiah is trying to create an alternative consciousness to break the culture of the day. We have to change and allow ourselves to be freed of the concerns of the ego so that we can present to the world a vision of society where seeming contradictions can live in harmony with one another and where the need for competition and violence are vanquished. Isaiah talks of the lion lying down with the lamb. That is the call of the Church. We should be creating an alternative way of living. Instead we became the place, certainly in Western Europe, of right-winged conservatism which more and more people have abandoned. Our unwillingness to enter into deep radical change impels the prophet to say to the people of his day and to us 'Take your wrongdoing out of my sight, stop doing evil, learn to do good, search for justice, help the oppressed, plead for the widow'. That's liberation theology, straight from the mouth of the prophet Isaiah.

In chapter 1, verse 18, the prophet writes, 'Come now, let us talk this over. Though your sins are like scarlet, they shall be white as snow, though they're as red as crimson they shall be as wool, if you're willing to obey you shall eat the good things of the earth. The rebellious sons, the sword shall eat you instead.' Leprosy begins with small red spots, which eventually go white as they rot the flesh. Isaiah is saying very clearly, that we need to change or we will destroy ourselves and the world in which we live.

As Isaiah develops the prophet becomes filled with the concept of 'forever'. Up to the time of Isaiah the people of Israel have not had any sense of 'forever'. For a lot of Jewish people time is now, life when it ends, ends, but Isaiah has experienced a 'forever father' an overwhelming and everlasting love. Metanoia only happens when we turn and face the reality of love. It doesn't seem to matter how often we hear that call, we run away from love; and yet acknowledging love is the only way to that deep inner change. It is amazing how often 'everlasting' and 'forever' are used in the writings of Isaiah. It seems as though the prophet has experienced something within that he understands eternity.

Isaiah then begins to explore what that might mean using images of the highway of holiness. The highway that the redeemed are going to go down, that has no end. But it is interesting that it always starts in the now. The redeemed of the Lord will experience that redemption in the here and now and forever. If we are beginning to believe that we are the redeemed of the Lord and are living like the redeemed in justice and integrity, in the knowledge of a forever loving God, then he reminds us that what we have is a gift. We have not done this in our own strength. Metanoia is always the gift of God. Isaiah begins to use overwhelming pictures of the greatness of God, before whom we are nothing. Isaiah has been overpowered by God and has experienced something that we have probably not experienced; the absolute momentous character of who God is.

The prophet knows that promises energise people. That is why he uses so many images, constantly setting promises before them, promises that he himself has experienced and fulfilled in his own heart. In chapter 25, Isaiah gives the promise of the messianic banquet. Despite all the prophet has said, there is much to hope for in Israel's relationship with God. When we turn and face love and are propelled into metanoia, we begin to know the truth that our hope lies in God. Much of the rest of Isaiah is a theology of hope. The Prophets never stop hoping. They will never throw out the promise; hope is not just wishful thinking, it is believing the promise. It is an attitude of mind and heart; it is a way of being in the world. It is always about expanding your horizon. When God shuts the way ahead, you turn to the right. When the right closes down, you turn to the left. There are a lot of people who try to plan for God and when nothing happens they lose hope. Hope keeps us believing, keeps widening our horizons.

In chapter 35 Isaiah says that if we have entered into the changing transforming power of love then we will believe the promise of God 'The wilderness and the dry lands exalt. Let it bring forth flowers, let it sing and rejoice. Courage, do not be afraid, your God is coming; he is coming to save you. The eyes of the blind shall be open, the ears of the deaf unsealed, the lame shall leap like a deer and the tongues of the dumb shout for joy'.

Those who are undergoing metanoia will always hear the call to serve the world. There is no way that God will ever give up on the world or on humanity. God wanted to create the world. God wanted you to be created because God is love. The experience of metanoia will always free us from those things that stop us believing that to be true and from those things that stop us serving the world. Metanoia means that we will always be filled with the compassion and love of God, which ultimately means that we will give our lives for the sake of the world. Metanoia makes us a sign of contradiction in the world because we live in a bigger picture; God's picture, which fills us with hope, peace and joy. We have discovered that our lives are not our own. It means that we can step outside the systems that surround us because we don't need them to create our identity or give us our security. It is then that we can, in the power of God, create, in the words of Paul VI, 'a society of sharing, solidarity, and love.'

CHAPTER NINE

JESUS - THE MODEL FOR METANOIA

When I was training to be a priest, the Liverpool students used to meet with the then Archbishop of Liverpool, Derek Worlock. During the gathering we would always have some input from an outside agency to broaden our awareness. In 1980 our vocations director brought to the gathering a woman who was hugely influential in charismatic renewal in Ireland and in the north west of England. She was a woman of forthright opinions about the church, about Priesthood, and about the dignity of the all the baptised. She was fearless as she spoke about all these things. She also spoke of the need for a personal relationship with the Lord and for a new awareness of the Spirit in our lives. I have to say it went down like a lead balloon and all the criticism and anger fell on those few students involved in Charismatic Renewal.

I decided that I would have to go and speak to her. I said that I felt it would be wise to pull back slightly and try and win people on side with gentleness rather than a full-frontal attack with all guns blazing. She listened very graciously to what I had to say and then smiled at me and said 'go away and read Galatians 1:10 and if you still feel the same way come back to me and we will talk again.' When I read the quotation from Galatians my jaw hit the floor. This is what I read 'So now whom am I trying to please - man, or God? Would you say it is men's approval I am looking for?' I had wanted people to experience the Lord and hear the Gospel, but not if it cost me. I wanted things to be safe and comfortable.

That experience taught me a valuable lesson. The gospel cannot be forced into the parameters that we want it to fit into and sometimes we have to take risks to proclaim the Good News. Often what we do won't be seen as acceptable or even orthodox, but whose approval are we looking for?

I think I learnt the lesson, but I don't think as Church that we have. We keep Jesus locked up and safe. This man who is supremely free, filled with the wildness of the Spirit, who knows no guile in the way he acts or responds to people and we try and tame him and domesticate him. I think it is because he is the model for what we are supposed to be and if we can keep him safe and respectable, all the better for us. Yet he is the supremely free person who in his humanity, having had a life-changing experience of God in the desert, lived as the son of God. He did this to show us how to live as sons and daughters of God. It is almost as though God has said, 'You don't understand what I am calling you to be. You don't understand freedom, so I am going to have to show you what it means.' What it meant for Jesus was crucifixion, death.

I think we pay lip service to metanoia and the freedom that it brings. We bandy around words like transformation and change and even repentance without really being willing to let the Spirit take us where the Spirit wants. We doubt Jesus being fully human because if he is fully human then we know that we are not. When the chips are down we are so caught up with ourselves that it is too scary to move into the whole area of metanoia and transformation and to become who we really are in God because it brings with it conflict. When we taste that freedom of who we are in God that metanoia brings, then we become scary people. Why? I think it is because we put a mirror up to the face of the world and the world doesn't like what it sees and inevitably will hate the one who holds the mirror.

To embrace the freedom that is in the heart of God for us is a difficult walk. To know that we are loved with an intensity and passion that became flesh in Jesus and which sets us free from sin and darkness, and to allow that truth to transform us so that we become free people living out our lives as children of God, is not an easy thing to do. It wasn't easy for Jesus and it won't be easy for us.

I often think we avoid metanoia by creating our own version of Jesus and his Gospel, a version that we can handle and cope with. Don't make Jesus into something he's not so that you don't have to make the journey. Don't make him into what you want him to be so that you don't have to change the way you live. Let him show you what a transformed person is all about and then if you choose to walk away, so be it. That is what the rich young man did and it was okay but don't present to the world a parody of the Gospel where you can be just like everyone else with the add on that you go to Church on a Sunday and maybe live by a particular moral code. There is more to life for the believer always more.

Each of the synoptic Gospels gives us an account of the Baptism of Jesus. We don't really know what happened but whatever it was he came out of the experience knowing that he was loved by God in a way he had never imagined. In terms of what we have been talking about, he came out of the desert having had an experience of metanoia and the incredible freedom it brought. He had encountered God and knew that he was a child of God. The Spirit who drove him into the wilderness let him sense his true self. Jesus' life then was lived out inviting others into that same freedom that he experienced.

It was a freedom in which he knew that he was loved by

God and that every human person who walks this earth is loved by God. So he did all in his power to free people from those things that held them captive. Healing is a product of love and Jesus allowed the love that was in the heart of God for humanity and which was in him, to flow through him. It was almost as if he was saying to the people that he met 'can you not sense your dignity, can you not sense the love that is in the heart of God for you?'

6-1-15

He was full of joy at the sheer gift of being alive. He was present to the moment, not caught up with what had been or what might be, simply present. Why oh why have we turned Jesus into this serious, almost lugubrious, individual who is somehow removed from life? He didn't sit in a corner with a halo round his head. I think he laughed and drank and told his stories. He was a man full of humour and joy. He was asked to party after party. He was free to be full of joy because he wasn't caught up in all the stuff that we get caught up in. He wasn't anxious about what others thought of him. He was free to delight in the presence of anyone he met. He was never constrained by the expectations of others or the limitations that others tried to put on him. Metanoia really does free us to live in the moment and enjoy the gift of it without being worried or frightened of what others will think.

Jesus had encountered God and therefore could allow the

presence of God within him to widen his heart and mind
so that he could accept and love those who were seemingly
unacceptable. Even that negates the way Jesus acted
because for him no-one was unacceptable. It wasn't that
he knew that they were unacceptable and loved them
anyway. He just didn't live by or even understand the
differentials we put on people. People were simply people
who needed to know they were loved by God. Whether
you were Nicodemus, Joseph of Arimathea, or a woman
who was considered unclean, you were treated in the same
way. I was recently trawling the web and came across a
Parish website that was for me wonderful to behold and
filled me with delight. It invited anyone and everyone to
be part of the worshipping community. It named
categories of people who were welcome and all of them
were groups of people who, for whatever reason, might feel
alienated by the Church. No-one in the sight of God
should ever be labelled as unacceptable or unworthy.

Jesus was free to be angry at the state that religion had got
people in to. Without that encounter with God he would
not have dared take on the Scribes and the Pharisees and
the temple authorities. He would have been too afraid, too
anxious about what might happen to him. But you see
Jesus had nothing to protect because metanoia had
happened within him and he lived with an awareness of
God's agenda. I am a great admirer of those who are free

enough to be able to face Church authorities in the truth and the light of the Gospel. It takes great courage to challenge the Church, especially when you rely upon the Church for your life. I am often saddened by the response they get but always heartened by the willingness to do it. I often pray for courage myself to stand for what I believe to be true without worrying about the consequences.

One of the most beautiful passages in John's Gospel is the passage about the raising of Lazarus. It is beautiful because it shows the compassion and vulnerability and sensitivity which comes from living out of the metanoia experience. Jesus weeps over the death of Lazarus. How many of us are free enough and willing to weep even when something terrible has happened to us. Jesus was free to weep even over the city that he loved. Weeping is seen, certainly in the Western world, as a sign of weakness and a lack of control when in fact it shows real strength and emotional depth.

One of the greatest signs of whether metanoia is happening within you is that of forgiveness. If you look at Jesus you'll find him able to forgive to such a degree that it's almost frightening. Remember as he hangs on the Cross the words, 'Father forgive them for they don't know what they're doing.' It is only someone who has encountered the reality of God and let that reality mould

him and shape him, who can give away his life with a word
of forgiveness. I have been humbled and honoured on
many occasions to hear incredible stories of forgiveness.
I have met people who have gone to into Prisons to forgive
their children's murderers because of the Gospel and its
power in their lives.

A few months ago I was in the centre of Liverpool and
bumped into an old teacher of mine. I have to say that I
froze and didn't quite know what to do or what to say.
When I was at school the man was known as the butcher.
I was terrified of him and very much aware as a child of
the amount of anger and violence within him. I can
remember him one day picking up a child in front of me
and banging his head on the ceiling for some insignificant
misdemeanour. Thank God that can't happen in schools
now, but when I met him that day I was filled with an anger
and bitterness that I didn't even know was there. When he
spoke to me he told me that he had given up teaching some
years earlier and he asked me could I forgive him for all
the pain he had inflicted on children down the years. He
held out his hand and looked steadily at me and thank
goodness I was able to find within the strength to say yes.
I remember at the time feeling an incredible freedom.
Forgiveness is the greatest sign of living in the kingdom,
the greatest sign of metanoia.

To live in the freedom of the children of God will lead us into conflict with the systems of this world which threaten to overwhelm people. It will mean that issues of justice cannot be overlooked. That freedom will invite us into the ways of compassion and love and mercy and forgiveness but like Jesus you will be misunderstood and laughed at and rejected but you will know life in the most incredible glorious way and you'll begin to understand eternity.

Jesus is our model for what it means to live the transformed life, the freed life, the life that is in touch, but he challenges us to know who we are in God's sight and to be willing to let God use us to bring salvation to the world.

CHAPTER TEN

RELATIONSHIP MATTERS

Several years ago I went to Russia on holiday. I have always been fascinated by the Romanov dynasty and particularly the story of what happened to the Tsar Nicholas and Alexandra his wife and their children. I have also been intrigued by tales of the mad monk Rasputin. The other reason I wanted to go was to see the Hermitage which is full of spectacular works of art and particularly to spend some time in front of Rembrandt's picture of the Prodigal Son. We set off for Poland where we were to meet the group we would be travelling with and had some wonderful experiences on the way through Belarus into Russia.

I remember laughing loud and long at the shock on an American woman's face at the hotel in Belarus. She asked for more coffee at breakfast. The waitress fixed a long hard stare on her face and said 'No' and then walked away leaving the woman horror struck. We visited an old lady's house so we could see how Russia's farming population lived. It was a shack and very dirty but what struck me most was the dignity of the woman who lived there. She sat upright on a wooden chair and smiled graciously at us as we trooped into her house. I hope she was paid well.

We spent some time in Moscow looking at the Kremlin and the various sites around the city and then travelled by a huge train to St Petersburg which is the most beautiful of cities. I was able to indulge my fascination with what happened to the Tsar and his family and hear more stories of the mad monk. The day finally came when we were to visit the Hermitage.

As I drew near the gallery Rembrandt's picture was in, I could feel myself getting more and more excited until finally I stood before the picture with its rich colours glowing. The mercy and compassion of the father welcoming back the son, just flowed from it. I was transfixed. If I could have stayed there for a day I would have done. I had read Henri Nouwen's book on the Prodigal Son some years before this experience and I could see why he took a year visiting the picture every day. It was a profound experience of who God is and of the loving parental care of God. It was a moment when I realised again that our relationship with God is all that matters.

I am becoming more and more aware that where metanoia happens is primarily within our relationship with God.

Our limited understanding of God and our refusal to be open to the more, is the biggest sin of humanity because it can cause us to take act in a way that is diametrically opposed to the God we say we worship. That then effects everything else, our relationship with the world we live in and with our brothers and sisters. Metanoia invites us to meet love face to face and to know that despite our sin and despite the brokenness of our lives, love is enough. God is bigger and more than we can ever imagine. I sometimes think it is such good news that we can hardly believe it, so we begin to put limitations on it and reduce the incredible gift of love that transforms and frees, to being dependent on us.

If you look at the Gospels they all present a different face of Jesus and ultimately the call to metanoia in each Gospel is slightly different. In Luke's Gospel the call is to change so much that we begin to love the poor and the broken. In Matthew's Gospel, it is that the Gospel so impacts our lives that we can only be merciful and compassionate. For Mark, metanoia means to change so much that we understand and embrace suffering for the sake of the world. When we read that little word 'repent' at the beginning of each of the synoptic Gospels I doubt that we realise it means so much.

For John, metanoia is all about the depth of our

relationship with God. Dare we believe in the immensity of love that stops us in our tracks, turns us around, and invites us to see differently? When Jesus in John's Gospel meets the first disciples he simply says, 'Come and see'. He doesn't say, get your lives sorted and then come. He doesn't say, beg for forgiveness and in my magnanimity you will receive it. He simply says, 'Come and see'. No requirements, no conditions, just invitation. Come and discover who I am, come and see what I have to offer. He doesn't teach them academically but invites them to share with him. I often wondered what they shared, what they saw.

I think it has something to do with being real. The disciples saw in this man someone with whom they could share their pain and brokenness and know that it was okay. They could be real, without their masks, and know that they were all right. That's what gave them life, and when you find that in someone you stick with them and you begin to share what you find with others. They met compassion and mercy and love in a human being in a way they'd never met it before and would never meet again.

In her book Blessings, Mary Craig describes what it was like taking her son Paul to Lourdes. Paul was very badly disabled. He was so disfigured that people could hardly look at him. One day Mary took Paul to the Blessed Sacrament procession and as the Bishop brought the monstrance around the sick to bless them the most incredible hush settled on the crowd. In the depth of the silence Paul began to cackle and Mary said for a moment it sounded like a maniac was loose and she was filled with shame and stood there not knowing what to do. Suddenly through the crowd pushed an old French woman; with tears streaming down her face she lifted Paul out of his chair and held him up to be blessed. In that compassionate action Mary said she saw the face of God. When you meet compassion and mercy and love you're never quite the same again.

The Disciples were never quite the same again. Metanoia in John's Gospel is all about the process of relationship. We have to have the courage to let God be God and break through the petty limitations that we put on love. The truth is that when the chips are down it is all about love; the uncontrollable love of the creator for the created.

The gospel of John is different from the others. The word 'synoptic' comes from a Greek word which means to see with the same eyes. The synoptic Gospels use more or less similar material with some differences. John uses completely different material, the origin of which we don't know. His material is written at many different levels.

Throughout the Gospel the words are both on a practical level and on a spiritual level. It's this latter level that John is more interested in. He uses misunderstanding scenes to lead us from one level to the other.

For example, the scene with Nicodemus shows very clearly the different levels the Gospel speaks at. Nicodemus asks at the human level, 'How can a man be born again?' Jesus answers at a spiritual level. Nicodemus is being challenged to come and see and discover a God who is more than he could ever imagine. John invites us all the time to move to a deeper understanding. He frequently uses double meanings; for example the crippled man cured at the pool of Siloam has an encounter with love and is then challenged to share love. The word 'Siloam' means sent. The whole story can be read as a teaching on Discipleship. If you're not aware that he uses double meanings then the story of the man at the pool of Siloam is the story of the cure of a crippled man and nothing else.

All the time when reading the Gospel you have to ask yourself what John means by writing that. The Gospel was written to speak to the heart and not just to the intellect. It is to reveal the truth of a loving God, whose love is far greater than our finite minds can ever begin to comprehend. That truth about love is at the heart of metanoia. It will change our lives if we can dare to let go of our image of a small-minded God who demands moral rectitude before bestowing love upon us. 9 - 1 - 15

The Gospel of John is not just an intellectual exercise, although intellectually it is quite an incredible piece of writing. The heart and mind must both be engaged as we look at the truth that it reveals. Apparently there are two words in Greek that mean time. The first is 'chronos' which is indicative of a time-line. For example, I was born in..., then I..., then I... . John discards that. He really is not interested in what happened and the order in which it happened. The second word is 'kairos', which means the significance of the moment. John writes his Gospel to let us know the significance of the moments and he organises facts and puts into the mouth of Jesus the words that let us know the significance of the moment. The Gospel was written some years after the death of Jesus. Exact words and incidents can't be remembered. What *is* remembered is the significance of the moment and it's that which is inspired It's that which has significance for us now.

The message of the Gospel is very clear. Jesus is the Son of God, who is the source of eternal life. Any good Jew would know, when reading the Gospel, what Jesus was saying when he begins his long monologues with 'I am'. In Jewish tradition only God can claim 'I am'. Go back to the Book of Exodus and you find God revealed as 'I am' to Moses in the story of the burning bush. John is telling us that Jesus is God. The God who pre-existed time, the God who is always in the present; the God who is love and who invites us into a mind blowing relationship where love is poured out, lavished upon the beloved. It is an incredible claim that spreads from the prologue to the end of the Gospel. Jesus says, 'I am the Bread of Life'. 'I am the Light of the world.' 'I am the Good Shepherd.' 'I am the Way Truth and Life.' 'I am the Resurrection and the Life.'

As if to re-inforce who Jesus is, John shows how all the major Religious feasts have been replaced by him. The feasts no longer have any relevance. Jesus is the one who reveals this God of love. The Jewish background of symbolism legalism and ritualism has been replaced by new Spiritual moments where we can encounter the depth of love that turns us around in our tracks and makes us see in a completely different way. In chapter 2, at the wedding feast of Cana, we find the ritualism of purification replaced by the new wine of Salvation, the only thing that can really cleanse us and set us free. In chapter 3 we find Jesus replacing the temple with his own body. That must have really scandalised the Jewish readers; the temple was the centre of their lives and here was this man telling them that it was no longer important, that only Jesus was important. What is John saying to us? Don't sink your hope in the material, don't make your Churches an end in themselves. It is the person of Jesus that matters. Have we really learned the lesson?

In chapter 3, Jesus shows how birth into the chosen people has nothing to do with circumcision and ritualism but it is a spiritual reality, dependent on God alone. Metanoia is a gift. It never depends on the recipient. It is simply gift, not dependent on morality or church attendance, but gift. In chapter 4, in the dialogue with the Samaritan woman we find Jesus breaking down the Jewish provincialism which said that God could only be worshipped in Jerusalem. When metanoia begins to happen within us we begin to see and know that God is everywhere. In chapter 5, we begin the breaking down of the Jewish feasts. Jesus is the Sabbath. We will only find rest in him.

In chapter 6, he replaces the Passover, 'I am the Bread of Life'. He is freedom, he is salvation. He declares himself the light of the world and the living water in chapters eight and nine, replacing the symbolism used at the feast of tabernacles. In chapter 10, we find the feast of the dedication of the temple replaced as Jesus himself is dedicated.

John is inviting us into something extraordinary with this Jesus. All the time he is moving Religion from the level of institutionalism to the level of the personal. Get to know Jesus, John is telling us, and you will understand that he is all that matters. It is the personal all the time. I wonder quite often whether or not we have slipped into the same place the Jews were in when John's Gospel was written. We have replaced the personal with the institutional and so it is our buildings that matter, it is dogma, it is doctrine, it is ritual. It is not that those things don't matter but the priority is always to experience relationship with a living loving God. John tells us again and again that it is the personal that matters. It is all about relationship that reveals the reality of God, so turn around and face love.

I think we avoid relationship with a living God because the personal is the scariest place to live. It makes demands on us and makes us face reality. Enter into a really deep relationship with someone and live with the tension that it can bring. It is far easier to live at the level of institutionalism. Finally, at the end of Chapter 10, Jesus describes himself as the fullness of life. If you want real life you will only find it in Jesus. So for John, metanoia, even though he never uses the word, is implicitly about entering into relationship with a God who can only love and whose love will sweep us off our feet and help us see things completely differently.

CHAPTER ELEVEN
THE CRY OF THE POOR

Forty years ago I was part of a huge prayer group that met in the Notre Dame Convent in Mount Pleasant in Liverpool. Some weeks there were over a hundred people there of all sorts of persuasions. There were some people who lived on the streets there were some who came from affluent parts of Liverpool and everything in between. One of the people who regularly used to join us was a bag lady called Thora.

I can still see her now with a small velvet hat on her head encased with dirt, a matted tweed coat that was several sizes too big for her and an array of bags in which she carried all her possessions. Her face and hands were ingrained with grime and she had just two teeth in her mouth that always looked as though they were about to fall out. She was a sad little woman who always arrived after the meeting had started. She would then take ten minutes to settle down and eventually when she was still she would begin to cry. She sat and cried week in, week out, saying that she was a backslider and there was no hope for her.

One particular Friday night she arrived with her bags and settled down. After a while she seemed a bit agitated and suddenly stood up and burst into tears then she shouted at the group and said 'Are all your nice words for me as well as all the others'? There was no immediate answer, probably because of shock, and so she picked up her bags and went out.

I have never forgotten that incident because I think in a sense it has challenged me to ask myself the question 'Who is the Good News for?' Is it just for the nice Religious people who know all the right words and the right phrases and who sit and stand at the right times during Church services or is it also for those who are hurting and broken?

Luke has Jesus situated with those who are on the edges and he challenges us to let go of all our attempts to be good religious people. He wants us to be real. It is the most scandalising piece of writing because it says that in God's eyes all are of value and all are welcome. For Luke, metanoia is about that inner transformation that means we look at every person regardless of who they are and what they are and not just love them but be willing to spend time with them and to enjoy their companionship.

I was recently speaking at a retreat day in London. I had

been talking about falling into grace. I had said that we religious people have managed to reduce the gift of God into a prize to be earned, thinking the better we are the more we'll get. I went on to say that if that was what we thought we could not be more wrong. The invitation of God is to live in that free place of love poured out and received which always means to live in a world of abundance and open horizons. Most of us live in small petty worlds where our own ego is the only reality that motivates us. We spend most of our time striving to get more of God and God has already done it. God has given Godself away. The love of God is poured out. We are forgiven, freed, saved. The heart of God is love flowing out and there is nothing we can do to earn it. We just simply fall into grace. That is what converts us and changes us and enables us to open our hearts to others. In terms of this chapter, for Luke that is radical metanoia.

Afterwards a man came up to me and said that he had found what I said terribly difficult to take. 'After all,' he said, 'if you take what you said to the extreme then heaven is full of bad people and people who have made mistakes and people who commit the worst kind of sins.' I looked at him and I felt so sad because he had not allowed the truth of the Gospel to penetrate his own need to limit the grace of God to those he thought were acceptable.

Metanoia for Luke invites us to change so radically that we begin to know the grace of God is limitless and therefore those on the edges become our friends. The poor and the broken and the needy become the ones we choose to spend our time with. It challenges us to move beyond our neat religious boundaries and really love, as Jesus did.

To understand that radical call in Luke's Gospel we have to try and understand the temple politics of Jesus day. I have read that the temple of Jesus day was the centre of the economic system, the political system and the social system within Judaism. Put simply, those who could worship were acceptable within society and some of them held the power and those who could not worship were excluded from mainstream society. There were huge numbers of people excluded from temple worship who were therefore outside the systems that made Jewish society work. If you read the book of Leviticus you will find them listed there.

The uncompromising nature of Luke's Gospel, and the reason why those who follow him have to change so much, is that Luke's Jesus will sit down and share food with the outsider. You find Zaccheus and tax collectors and sinners and prostitutes all sharing food with Jesus. Luke's Jesus will raise the dead and heal the leper. Luke's Jesus will mix with Samaritans and Syro-Phoenicians. He will allow a woman with a haemorrhage to touch his cloak. By doing all these things Jesus makes himself unclean in the eyes of the Jewish authorities and therefore outside the system. It is clear that Luke is saying to anyone who is willing to listen, that no-one is unacceptable, no-one is irredeemable, no one is excluded from the heart of God.

A few years I was on a retreat with a group of Priests, one of whom said that for the Jubilee year he had put up in the Church a huge banner which read: This is the Lord's year of favour... Whatever has happened to you in the past, however you have been treated, whatever your lifestyle you are welcome here in this place. He said that the poster went on to list all those groupings who for one reason or another might feel unaccepted by the Church. He described how he put it up one Saturday morning and then waited for the balloon to go up. The first person to come into Church was a very old lady who stood looking at the poster for a long time and then said to Peter: 'Thank goodness someone understands the Good News.' He said it was worth some of the hassle he got afterwards for that one comment.   19-1-15

You see the truth is that the good news is indiscriminate. It is for all people whatever state their lives may be in but I often think we're not going to help people recognise it by deeming them unacceptable. I often wonder how many more groups of people the church can alienate, some groups of women, gay people, divorced and remarried, those who have children outside marriage. The Good News is for all people, not just the comfortable middle class who say their prayers and sit in Church on a Sunday. The proclamation of that Good News is the mission of Jesus and it's our mission too.

Luke makes that very clear when in Chapter 4 he has Jesus choose his hometown of Nazareth to tell people the programme for his mission. He chose the Sabbath when people gathered in the synagogue. Waiting to hear him would have been relatives, friends, and neighbours as well as other people who lived there. What he said must have been incredibly challenging to them and for him very frightening to proclaim. Jesus told them that the Spirit of the Lord had been given to him. Just like the prophets in the Old Testament, he was anointed for mission. Jesus said that his mission was to preach the Good News to the poor. Who are the poor? You might ask yourself.

There's a sense in which all of us are poor. In the depths of our being there is a poverty of spirit that only God can heal. All of us need to hear the Good News of a God who is love. All of us need to hear the Good News of a God who is compassionate. All of us need to hear Good News which cuts through the nonsense we surround ourselves with, and the masks that we wear and tells us we're loved as we are. We are the poor and Jesus wants to proclaim Good News to us without judgement, condemnation or expectation of anything in return.

But this Gospel is not just about us and the Lord. It also forces us into relationship with other people. For the Gospel to have any impact, we too have to be good news to the poor wherever we find them and whoever they may be. We too have to proclaim liberty to captives. We too have to set the down-trodden free. Too many of us judge and condemn those who for whatever reason find themselves at the bottom of the heap. Too many of us hide behind the cosy little life we have built for ourselves and forget the old adage that, 'There but for the grace of God go I.'

When we do for others what Jesus wants to do for us, then the world will see a people who stand together and work together for the salvation of the world. We'll not just be creating religions and making ourselves feel good by practising our faith. We'll be allowing the Good News to be a lived reality. We'll be making an impact on those around us.

Jesus came to proclaim Good News to the poor. Let's hear

that good news for ourselves and allow it to flow through us into the lives of others as we respond to others need for freedom.

I do not think we realise just how shocking Luke's Gospel was to the organised religion of the day. It turned every system upside down. It shook the very foundations of Judaism. As soon as you exclude anyone in Luke's Gospel, whoever they may be, Jesus will sit down beside them. Ask yourself whether or not you would sit down and have lunch with a prostitute?

Jesus must have been the most frustrating of men because he never did what was expected of him and his friends were the outcasts and the unclean. In a Church that seems to be a community for those who are acceptable and who live in an acceptable way maybe we have some lessons to learn from Luke's Jesus. Sadly, we love to have some people who are in and others who are out. I guess it makes us feel superior but it is never the Jesus way. Metanoia calls us to that place where our hearts are so broken and changed that we can embrace the poor, the broken, the street people, the refugee. Metanoia invites such radical change that we can love the gay person and those who struggle with their gender. Metanoia invites us to look with compassion on the murderer, the paedophile, the pornographer. Can we simply love them without demanding change from them or even sorrow for what they do or don't do?

These are huge questions that do not make comfortable reading but asking ourselves those questions leads us to that place where metanoia begins to happen and our hearts and minds become bigger and wider than they were before. It is not an easy process because it means we have to let go of many of our certainties about who is acceptable and who is not. It means we have to face the scorn of those who either cannot or refuse to see the amazing abundance of grace, and it means we have be willing to be seen with those regarded as less within society. I often think that the way of metanoia is the narrow road that Jesus talked of. It is easy to keep the rules and dismiss those who don't, or can't for whatever reason, as not being worthy. It is far more difficult to change within, so that we love those who seem to be unnacceptable. I love the quotation from Gustav Guttierez, the South American Liberation Theologian, who calls Luke's Gospel 'the gospel of the outsider'.

Luke's Jesus will challenge us to recognise that we are the outsiders despite our cover up attempts. We are all broken and have made mistakes and are in some senses on the edges and he will challenge us to open our hearts and minds to those who do not fit the norm, that is if we let him speak to us at all. Radical metanoia is the means by which we begin to see that grace is boundless and limitless and our role as Church and as individuals is to allow the grace of God to flow through us.

CHAPTER TWELVE

THE CALL TO COMPASSION AND MERCY

My grandmother lived in a street of back to back houses not far from Liverpool City centre. It was the place where my brother was born and I was almost born. At the bottom of the street lived Mrs Jackson who had several children all who had different fathers. It was a so-called respectable area and Mrs Jackson was frowned upon by most of her 'good living' neighbours.

In 1943 my nana's eldest child, May, died of TB. She was 23 and my grandparents and my mum and uncle were devastated. For a couple of days no-one knocked on their door. I guess no-one knew what to say but eventually the door knocker went and my mum went to open the door. There stood Mrs Jackson and just for a moment Mum didn't know what to do until Mrs Jackson put down the bag she was carrying and threw her arms around my mum who dissolved into tears. Mrs Jackson then picked her bag up and marched into the house and for the next week took over the kitchen and the cleaning.

Mum always said that from that day onward my nana would

always use the old phrase, 'you can't judge a book by its cover', and Mum said that she learned the lesson never to judge another person but to do what Richard Rohr calls 'holding the mystery'.

Megan McKenna has written a book called 'Matthew the Gospel of mercy.' Radical metanoia in Matthew's Gospel leads us to that place of mercy and deep compassion. It was that mercy and compassion that my mum and her family met in Mrs Jackson. The word compassion means 'to suffer with' and I have heard mercy defined as 'undeserved kindness'. Only deep metanoia can lead us to that place where we can be compassionate and merciful because only an encounter with the compassion and mercy of God turns us around to see that mercy and compassion are the only way for the Christian to live.

The Jerusalem bible calls Matthew's Gospel, 'The great Charter of a New Order' inaugurated by Christ. Matthew's community was overwhelmed that a whole new picture has been presented to them in terms of what life really means. It is the new order brought about by the life, death, and resurrection of Jesus. Things would never be the same again. This Jesus had turned the old order upside down.

Matthew presents Jesus as the new Moses and the law that

he gives is the law of mercy. The Gospel is structured very cleverly. It's full of allusions to the Old Testament and to Jesus as the new Moses. The Gospel is divided clearly into five books. They correspond to the five books of the Pentateuch again adding credence to Matthew's presentation of Jesus as the new Moses.

If we don't understand the First Testament we will never fully understand Jesus, who was a Jew and immersed in the ancient writings and customs of his people. At the heart of the book of Deuteronomy lies the Shema and what that meant. 'You must love the Lord your God with your whole heart and mind and understanding.' Without reflecting on the book of Deuteronomy we don't get a sense of how important that was to the Jews and how Jesus would have said it many times a day as he walked in and out of the houses in his village. He takes that Shema and turns it into something new, the law of love written on the hearts of those who enter metanoia.

The infancy narratives of Matthew's book are a prologue to the rest of the Gospel and they are almost pure theology and very little chronology. In the first few chapters, Matthew is trying very hard to tie up Jesus with the Jewish tradition while at the same time talking about the new order.

We begin the infancy narrative with a genealogy in which Matthew wants to show Jesus as the goal of history. Firstly, Matthew shows Jesus as the son of David, the son of Abraham. He wants to make us realise that Jesus comes from the tradition of Israel. He comes from the tradition of the Patriarchs, of Isaac and Jacob and Judah. This Jesus is part of human history, one of us.

By the time we get to the account of the massacre of the innocents, we find Matthew trying to connect Jesus to the massacre of all the elder sons when Pharaoh let the people out of Egypt. Jesus becomes the new Moses, leading the people out of slavery to freedom. Matthew has to find a way for Jesus to be the new Moses, and lead the people out of Egypt so he has to get him down to Egypt. And so Mary and Joseph go down, across the Negev desert into Egypt. A Jew who would understand the Old Testament would pick up the point immediately. Jesus is to be the new son coming out of Egypt into the Promised Land. Matthew uses the quote from Jeremiah, 'A voice was heard in Ramah, sobbing and loudly lamenting. It was Rachel, weeping for her children'. This is actually the lament at the time of the exile, so Jesus not only personifies the call out of Egypt but also he personifies the pain and the struggle that the people went through when they were sent into exile. So all this he is going to live out in his person.

In one human life he will live out the human struggle, the human emotion, the human doubt, the human faith, and the human pain of all of Israel. So we have the exodus and the exile summed up here in the second part of the second chapter. God went out of his way to save Moses now he's going out of his way to save Jesus.

We then jump a little into Chapters 5-7, where we have the fullest explanation of Jesus as the new Moses in what has become called the Sermon on the Mount. It's unlikely that it happened as it's written. Matthew gathers together the substance of Jesus' teaching and preaching. We are offered a number of sayings that often seem to have no obvious connection with each other. The unity of this sermon stems from the person of Jesus, unique source and teacher of wisdom. Matthew gives an impressive setting to the Sermon on the Mount.

In the Old Testament, God traditionally speaks from the mountain, which is his holy place. Matthew is reminding us who Jesus is and who is the architect of this new world order. He presents Jesus as the new Moses giving the new law of life. Jesus sits down, as did the Jewish rabbis, when they were teaching officially.

So we have then the eight Beatitudes which are as essential to the Christian life as the Ten Commandments have been for the Jewish way of life but they only happen within us when we have turned around and faced love. In some translations, the word 'blessed' is used and in others, 'happy'. These are really weak translations from the Greek word 'makarios', which expresses deep overwhelming gladness, joy, bliss.

Looked at closely these are very paradoxical commandments because they don't tell anyone what to do. They simply tell us what we will be like if we live in the Kingdom. We will be poor in spirit, pure in heart, merciful, gentle, and peacemakers. If we live in the kingdom we'll thirst for what is right whatever is thrown at us. We'll be immersed in the love of God, who will satisfy our hunger and thirst, and somehow in the living out we shall see God. Remember the invitation to see the Kingdom.

The Beatitudes take us beyond the commandments to a new way of relating to one another in a new world order. They take us beyond the mere fulfilment of rules which the commandments gave, to a life style based on vulnerability, self-emptying and co-operation. It's all about the radical turn-around that metanoia invites us into. If you meet Christians who talk of the ten commandments as the rule of life, you can guarantee that they haven't understood Jesus.

It's far more difficult to live in the way of the beatitudes than simply respond to rules. That's the Kingdom. To follow Jesus is to follow him out of the old legality of the world's systems and into the new reality of living a much larger truth. Again, that is what metanoia promises. It's about discovering God as life giver and not just law giver. Megan McKenna in her book 'Matthew, the Book of Mercy' says 'this is revolutionary, this demands far more than anything the prophets preached… and how do we react to these words with outright resistance, disbelief, rejection of Jesus' words, and their deeper intent.'

After the beatitudes Jesus then tells us that we are the 'salt of the earth and the light of the world'. What salt is to food the Christians are to the world. We should give a taste to life that would otherwise seem bland and insipid. But we can only give others a zest for life if we ourselves have a real taste for living. Light and dark are the universal symbols of good and evil. Jesus calls his followers to be light, a light that dispels the darkness of the world and the gloomy shadows that can sometimes overpower us. Light gives vision, colour, true perception. It brightens the way and shows up obstacles over which we would stumble in the dark.

The light of Christ is a light that shines first of all in our own hearts, and we must allow it to flood into our hearts, even into their most secret corners. With the light of Christ there should be no fear, for his light overcomes and destroys darkness. What radical change there needs to be within us as individuals and within our institutions, if we are to be light and salt. It is mercy and compassion that lights up people's darkness. It is the reaching into people's lives with forgiveness and understanding that gives others a zest for life.

Over and over again, Jesus invites us to go further than we've ever gone before. 'Love your enemies' must be one of the most revolutionary messages of all Jesus' teaching. Love those who hurt you. We can't do that by ourselves, we need the power of God, and so Matthew says, 'be perfect as your heavenly father is perfect'. With the power of God you can love perfectly even those who hurt you.

Then in the Lord's Prayer we're invited to enter into a whole new way of relating to God. The invitation is to relate to God as Jesus does. Abba. It's in that relationship that we pray for the coming of the Kingdom, when everyone will know that God is enough and our fruitless searching for fulfilment will be over. We are invited to pray for forgiveness, the greatest sign of the kingdom. It's such a simple prayer, focusing on God and God's providence, but it also reminds us that if we pray, our words and deeds have to reflect one another; 'forgive us our trespasses as we forgive those who trespass against us'. It is mercy and compassion again.

In the rest of the Sermon on the Mount, Jesus urges us to examine our scale of values and our priorities. He tells that our eyes should be like a lamp that gives light to our lives; if we are blind to the truth we shall live in darkness and actually mistake darkness for light. That is why we need metanoia.

He also reassures us that we should not worry or be anxious. This new relationship that we're invited into, this new world order, is about trusting God more than anything. God knows what we need even more than we know ourselves. It's not foolishness to trust God; it's to understand the only reality that lasts. That's how Jesus lived.

In Chapter 7 we have more hard-hitting statements about what it means to follow Jesus. Don't judge because judgement destroys the community. It stops people living. Jesus illustrates his commandment with the saying about the splinter and the plank. It is a simple fact that we do not see our own faults. And when we do, we quite often transfer what we see in ourselves onto others. It takes the heat off. Radical metanoia helps us to see ourselves and others as God sees us and then compassion and mercy are the only way.

The whole of Jesus teaching is then summed up in a
single sentence: Treat others as you would have them treat
you. Scholars call it the golden rule. It's another way of
saying 'Love your neighbour as yourself.' Whoever your
neighbour may be: the black man, the addict, gay
people - love your neighbour. What's the lesson? Accept
yourself and love yourself with all your faults and
weakness and brokenness, so that you can love others.

Jesus never claims that his way is easy and so he says the
way to life and of life is a struggle. It is a squeeze to get
in by the narrow gate and the road is one of hardship and
endurance. It's far easier to judge and criticise. It's far
easier not to love than love. Why we have presumed that
the narrow way is about sexual morality, I have no idea.

The only thing that matters is doing the Father's will. The
desire to do God's will is the essence of Jesus mission.
Richard Rohr says this when reflecting on discipleship:
'It is not anyone who says to me, 'Lord, Lord,' who
will enter the kingdom of heaven, but the person who
does the will of my father in heaven.' What counts is
listening to Jesus and letting him teach you how to live.
What counts is becoming his personal disciple—a word
which originally meant 'pupil' or 'learner'.

What counts is doing what Jesus teaches, both through

the scriptures and through personal contact in prayer and what Jesus teaches is always the will of God.

Matthew stresses that Jesus spoke with authority. He believed what he spoke and lived out his belief. So Jesus the new Moses, the new law giver, tells us it's about the heart and conversion of the heart to the way of the beatitudes, the way of compassion and mercy and love. He takes the old law and he supercedes it with a law that it written in our hearts and which becomes a way of living. Let metanoia happen within you and you will bring life to the world.

CHAPTER THIRTEEN

THE WAY OF THE SUFFERING SERVANT

S ome years ago, when I was a Parish priest, I received a phone call from a woman asking me if I would go and see her sister who was slowly drinking herself to death. The woman was crying and I sensed that there was more to the story. When I arrived at the address I had been given I found myself outside a luxury block of flats in the best part of town. I rang the intercom and there was no answer. I was just about to walk away when the front door clicked. I pushed it open and went in and found the number of the flat that I was going to. When I got to the front door it was open, so I went in. After a few moments of looking I found myself in the lounge and sitting in the chair was an elderly woman with a glass of neat gin in her hand and it obviously wasn't the first of the day.

I told her who I was and she said that I had better leave before she caused me any trouble, so I sat down. She said nothing for a while and then her eyes filled up and she began to cry. Very haltingly her story began to take shape. She told me that she had been in a Prisoner of War camp where she had been raped on several occasions. When the war ended she was released from the camp an emotional and physical wreck. She had married twice and had five children but her experiences had damaged her badly and by the time she was in her forties both marriages had ended and she was drinking heavily.

She then met a man who was gentle and kind and she moved in with him thinking he would be the answer to her problems. She discovered too late that he was a drug dealer who was eventually murdered and since his death some twenty years earlier she hardly ever went out for fear of reprisals and was slowly but surely killing herself with alcohol. She told me that her children had abandoned her. Her two brothers and one of her sisters refused to see her. They thought she was a waste of space. Her neighbours ignored her because of years of noise and drunken behaviour. Her doctor refused to see her and social services had washed their hands of her.

The only contact with the outside world was the sister who had rung me. As she talked about that sister, her face softened and she smiled. She told me that this sister came every day and cooked and cleaned and washed. It was obvious that her sister gave an immense amount of support. She told me that her sister had paid the cost of her goodness. The rest of the family refused to speak to her or acknowledge her presence because they thought she was mad to try and help. When the woman's neighbours saw her coming to visit her sister, they waited for her to complain and often unleashed a barrage of profanity. Many times the sister had had the police on the doorstep and her life was very difficult. After a while I left, promising to comeback.

The next day was Sunday and I had just finished Mass when a woman approached me. It was the sister. I took her into the house and made her a cup of tea. She thanked me for visiting and for the promise to return. Eventually I asked her why she helped her sister in the face of all the criticism that she got. She looked and smiled and said, ' I love her; she's my sister and it's not really her fault.' Then she said, 'What sort of Christian would I be if I didn't help her. I'm willing to pay the cost.' I was so moved as I saw that this woman was willing to be discarded by her family and vilified by others for the sake of her sister.

Following the way that Jesus marks out for us will always involve suffering. We cannot avoid it. We will be rejected and treated as crazy people who don't understand the real world. It has little to do with the cares and worries that strike us during life and everything to do with being witnesses to the Jesus way. That's where Mark sees that metanoia has to happen. None of us willingly chooses suffering. No-one chooses rejection. No-one wants to be disregarded as a crazy, religious maniac. Nobody wants to die to themselves for the sake of others but that's what Mark sees as the life of those who follow Jesus. The work of the Spirit is to so fill us with awareness of the love of God that we will willingly go wherever we are led.

If you and I take on the values of love and compassion and begin to see every individual as a unique creation of God, then we will begin to suffer. Why? Because it will put us on the side of the little ones. It means we have to stand on the side of those most rejected by society, the asylum seeker, the refugee, the outcast, the aids sufferer, those who live on the edge. That will always cause conflict because to be on the side of the little one is to stand against those who have power or those who are frightened of losing what they think they have. That conflict, and the suffering and rejection that can come from it, is because of following Jesus.

If we begin to really live by the Gospel values of forgiveness and peace and understanding and acceptance then it will bring us into conflict with those who preach another way of life. If we begin to live simply and justly then we will begin to question the market forces that control society and allow some to starve while others live on the backs of the poor. The scorn of and the dismissal from others is a result of following the Jesus way.

To follow Jesus is an invitation to enter into the pain of the world, to enter into the needs of others and to help others find life in the death that they experience. It is an invitation to be on the side of the little ones and to experience suffering and rejection because of our willingness to stand for Gospel truth. That's not an easy way of living because it means we have to let go of our own desires and needs and learn how to really serve. It means that somehow we have to be willing to let our ego die, that force within us which would see everything as revolving around us. It is why we need metanoia.

Sadly, much of western Christianity is not willing to walk that way. Despite what we say about faith, we live in much the same way as many of those around us live, consumed by materialism and our need for power; living from a place of fear rather than a place of truth. We seem to have bought the values of the world and replaced a living dynamic faith with a piety that does nothing more than make us feel good. How can that be the Gospel of Jesus, the only way to find real life in its fullness? No, there will be conflict for those who follow the Jesus way and there will be suffering. There is the cross. Thank God faith tells us that taking up the cross is not the whole story. If it was we would die, we could not cope. If we face the cross then somehow our suffering will be transformed into glory just as Jesus' was, somehow each and every death we have to go through will give way to life. That is the promise of Jesus. We will be filled with joy and life that nothing and no-one can take away from us, not just in the future but in the here and now.

Mark's Gospel is obviously the simplest and the shortest of the gospels. It is largely a passion narrative aiming towards Jesus' crucifixion and the understanding of that crucifixion. What we can say for certain is that the author wants to prove to his community that Jesus is the Messiah, the anointed one. Mark wants us to see Jesus as the suffering servant who comes to the full knowledge of who he is, an experience of that divinity through the cross. Mark emphasises constantly Jesus as the suffering servant.

When Mark uses the word metanoia it is within that context. He doesn't want his reader to proclaim that Jesus is Lord too quickly or too lightly. We have to know what we are saying and its implications, because it implies that we are willing to go through darkness to find light, that we're prepared to go through suffering and death to find life. Without a radical encounter with a love that blows our minds away and turns us upside down, none of us would be willing to go down the path of suffering.

Most of us don't really understand the way of the Suffering

Servant. The only way to understand is to follow, to walk the Jesus way. So in Mark's Gospel Jesus takes twelve men with him and moves more deeply into the journey of faith, walking towards Jerusalem which symbolises for him 'the meaning of his life'. He invites his brothers to walk with him, to enter into the experience and through the experience know who God is. Mark seems to know that we will understand who God is for us when we see the crucified Lord. It is then that we will know that God is the eternal giver. That eternal pouring out of God is dramatically seen in the crucified Jesus. When we see Jesus on the cross we see him in his moment of loneliness but, ironically, his moment of Lordship. That brings us face to face with the true and terrible cost of knowing God, of intimacy and deep relationship with God. We see the cost that God is prepared to meet in order to show us love and life.

We begin to see the paradox that in order to live, we have to die. The glory Jesus speaks of often in the Gospels is the shameful, appalling death of a common criminal. I have certainly asked myself how can that be glory or triumph. How can a powerless victim of injustice be glorified? Jesus is glorified through all the suffering that he has to experience. It happens because he remains faithful and true to God's word of love and forgiveness, even forgiving those who nail him to the cross.

Failure for Jesus would have meant giving in to the values of this world. He could have cursed his enemies. He could have rallied his disciples and other followers to protect him with violence. He could have bemoaned his situation, protesting his innocence. It would have been easy in the circumstances to think only of himself and fight by every means to be freed. The triumph and glory of the cross shine out in the love that stays faithful whatever the cost may be; in the strength and certainty of a man who knows that he is loved by God and who is prepared to pay the cost of that love.

At the beginning of Mark's Gospel, Jesus is surrounded by people who love his miracles but as the Gospel progresses you find him moving out of the crowds to fewer and fewer people, because it costs to walk the Jesus way. Finally at the foot of the cross there is no one who is able to confess that 'Jesus is Lord' except, ironically, a pagan centurion. One person in Jesus' moment of absolute loneliness is free to see that Jesus is Lord.

The challenge Mark is giving us is to see in brokenness and suffering the presence of God. To see God in the people suffering in Palestine, Syria, Iraq, and countless other places. To see God when lives are devastated by bereavement and scandal and illness. When we have learnt to recognise God in the mess of humanity then we have entered into the Jesus experience, which is not logical or even understandable. Only the journey can help us to understand it.

So for Mark, metanoia is the willingness to turn and face the reality of love and take on what it means to follow Jesus. In Mark's understanding it has little to do with saying that we are sorry for our sins and everything to do with letting God's love break us for the sake of the world. For Mark it is about suffering, because that is what Jesus did to show us the face of God. I suppose the challenge for us is whether or not we are willing to pay the cost.

CHAPTER FOURTEEN

THE WORD THAT TRANSFORMS

I was in my third year at the seminary when I met Steve. He was a priest appointed to the staff as part of the Pastoral Department. The Pastoral Department was made up of a group of people whose job it was to help the students reflect on their pastoral work and on theology so that each individual could develop a Pastoral theology. From the moment he joined the department Steve and I hit it off and we spent a great deal of time together in and out of college. He was a larger than life personality full of good humour, gregarious, and outgoing. He took me to party after party and I met some wonderful people through him. He was also incredibly reflective seeking out the presence of God in every encounter he had. He would often say to me where have you met God today? His honesty was painful at times but even when his honesty confronted me with my weakness and fear I knew that he would help put me back together again. We shared an awful lot together and because of him my perspective was widened and he encouraged me to dream dreams for myself and for the Church. After I was ordained we still continued to meet together and Steve would challenge my ways of thinking; always pushing me to broaden my horizons, and I him. Steve eventually left the active ministry and married but he continued to be a force for good in my life. He died very suddenly in Ireland and even today I still miss his humour and his belief in me as well as his ability to make me think deeply about myself my life and the Church.

I suppose most of us can point to encounters with people that have changed our perceptions and made us see more clearly. Those meetings may have enabled us to move on to a new place in our lives and reminded us that God is always with us; always present, even when it doesn't seem so. For me such occasions and relationships are encounters with the risen Jesus, the one who became and becomes flesh, who lived and lives among us. Encounters with the Lord will always involve the opportunity for metanoia change and conversion.

The Scriptures are full of such meetings with the risen Jesus. I love the story of John's account of breakfast on the shore. Peter still gets it wrong and yet there is still the chance of a new beginning. The two disciples on the road to Emmaus are turned round and sent back to Jerusalem, the very place they had run away from and were terrified of. Mary of Magdala had to move beyond her own feelings of despair and brokenness in order to recognise the presence of the Lord; the one she initially thought was the gardener. Thomas had to be willing to see more clearly.

The rest of the disciples had to be willing to recognise the risen Christ and respond to him. It took them a while but the stories in the Acts of the Apostles help us to realise that respond they did. They are all metanoia moments, a turning round took place so that life could never be the same again. The previous four chapters of this book have been reflecting on the subtle differences each of the evangelists have in their accounts of the life of Jesus. We begin to see how wide-ranging and challenging metanoia is. Can we really enter into a deep relationship with the Lord that matters more than anything else? Is it possible to change enough to become friends with those who live on the edges? Can I let go of my own need in order to take on the pain and suffering of the world? Will I ever recognise that mercy and compassion are the core values of what it means to follow Jesus? Can I die to myself for those values? These are huge questions to reflect on and indeed they are part of the turning round, the metanoia.

Reflecting and praying through the Scriptures will by their very nature propel us into the process of transformation, personally, socially, politically, and economically. These Scriptures are all about metanoia, about being trans-formed in every way possible. If you don't want to change

then don't read the Bible. If you are happy with your
own way of doing things and your own views and
understandings, don't read the Scriptures. If you are
comfortable with doing Religious things, and building
up your own ego by doing them, then don't read the
Scriptures.

Transformation is not an easy road to travel and in fact
it is one that most of us avoid at all costs. We do not want
to have to face how we spend our money or how we
vote. Nor about areas of acceptance, forgiveness, love, or
compassion, because they make us feel vulnerable and
uncomfortable. We seldom want to mix with people who
do not fit in with our narrow understandings of how
people should be. If we are reading them as the Word of
God, the Scriptures will force us to look at our inner lives,
face our bitterness, our anger, our ultimate selfishness,
and allow those realities to be transformed. They will
encourage us not to run away from pain and sorrow but to
find life in them. Those areas are precisely where the
Scriptures are pointing us and we avoid going there
because it is costly.

Many years ago I met a woman in Shrewsbury. Her name
was Miriam and she had decided that she would sell her
house and go to Africa because the Word of God had
challenged her to go to the poorest of the poor. It was a

costly thing to do. She burned all her boats in this country but because of her faithfulness to what she believed to be God's word to her, hundreds of children have been educated who otherwise never would have been and the poorest of the poor have become her friends and her family.

The Scriptures will always challenge us to trust in God more than ourselves. They will confront us with our own smallness and our own greatness. They will defy us to be comfortable and inspire always to be open to change. They will invite us to live in the tension of the finite and the infinite. You will become a new creation if you allow the Scriptures to become life to you. Metanoia will happen. 2.7-1-15

This encounter with God can take us to places we never dreamed possible. We can experience an inner freedom and an inner security beyond our wildest dreams. We can find love that will take our breath away and make life vibrant and thrilling. The Church teaches us that the Scriptures are inspired by the Holy Spirit. Generations of believers have discovered that these books are alive and that somehow when we reflect on them and pray through them they have a power to lead us into the whole process of transformation. Many years ago a friend of mine heard the phrase from Matthew's gospel, 'Come to me all who labour and are overburdened and I will give you rest', as though she had never heard it before. Her reflection and prayer took her into a large and difficult council estate where she opened a drop-in centre for those who were burdened and for many years it was a haven and refuge for many people. All because one woman took the word of God, reflected on it, and allowed it to transform her.

Apparently, the word Gospel that we translate as Good News was a word taken from a culture where war and battles were accepted as the norm and a Gospel was a message of victory that announced a new beginning. These Scriptures are to enable us to have a radical new beginning every time we read them and pray through them. Do you allow the Word of God to lead you into metanoia each and every time you read them? I am sure you have heard it said that only those on the journey can really share the journey with others. What is the journey about? I think it is about amazement. Are you amazed by the God you meet in the Scriptures, or are you so familiar with these ancient books that you have lost your capacity to allow them to transform you? Do you know so much about the Scriptures, so much information that you can't let them transform you, because you think information is all it is about? Or are you so amazed by the God you encounter that you begin to see with a new set of eyes?

The relationship with God that the ancient peoples experienced is timeless. So their journey becomes our journey, their story our story. It is about encountering God and about transformation. If you are not on a journey with God you will not understand the call the Scriptures are giving to enter into the process of transformation. To pray the scriptures as the word of God is to enter into the process of metanoia. In order to allow that to happen we have to let go of popular misconceptions about the bible. The Bible is not primarily a history book, a moral handbook or a manuscript to prove that God exists. It is the faith story of a people called to grow in trusting and listening to the God who walks with us. Sadly, many people are afraid of God and often try to control God or manipulate God into being what we want God to be. The Bible is supposed to so amaze us that we fall in love with God and then everything is up for grabs. We will go where God leads and be open to doing what God wants us to do.

The living word of God draws us into an experience of God, an encounter with God where we know that God is alive and with us. It draws us into metanoia. Rosemary Haughton, a feminist theologian, says this encounter is 'A knife-edge of experience'. Richard Rohr says, 'Outside an experience of this kind of God most religion will remain merely ritualistic, moralistic, doctrinaire, and largely unhappy.' The Bible wants to draw us into an experience of God that is beyond our finite minds and yet which frees us to see and believe and hope and love. How are you going to respond? Are you going to trust? Are you going to risk? Are you willing to look stupid and foolish in order to journey and discover?

Many years ago I met a Pentecostal minister named Ruth Heflin. She was an incredible woman, whose ministry spread across the world. She lived in Jerusalem with a huge community and ran youth camps in America. She had travelled extensively across Europe. On several occasions she met world leaders, presenting herself as someone with a message from God. She said the strange thing was that she always got an audience and her message was always the same; choose the things that bring life for yourself and for the people that you serve. Ruth died a couple of years ago and I have heard that there were several heads of state at her funeral, simply because of the effect she had on them. The point is not whether she really had a word from God for them, although I have no doubt she did. The point is that the Gospel had so turned Ruth around that she did not mind how foolish she looked or what happened to her as long as she was faithful to what she believed to be true.

If you read the Scriptures asking the right questions, like

'What is this telling me about myself or about God?' 'What is this saying about my life?'; if you're asking questions like, 'Is God real?' 'Can life be different than it is?' 'Can the Kingdom happen now?' 'Can I encounter God now?' 'Am I being transformed?' then maybe you will begin to get a foothold into what the Bible is about. If you are on a journey of trying to listen and trust you will begin to understand. When I read the Scriptures I always pray for the enlightenment of the Holy Spirit before I read. I always have a good commentary with me to enable me to understand the culture in which particular books were written and I pray that, whatever is revealed to me, I will be willing to respond whatever the cost. Over the next three chapters I am going to reflect on what I think are the three main fruits this entering into metanoia might bear in our lives. They are simplicity, joy, and gratitude and they enable us to become a blessing for the world.

CHAPTER FIFTEEN

SIMPLICITY - A FRUIT
OF METANOIA

Daniel was a gentleman who used to come into the Chaplaincy at Liverpool University for some warmth, some food, and a drink. Sometimes Daniel was lucid and witty, other times he was as confused and as bewildered as it is possible to be. When he was in that state of being he was impossible to talk to or, when angry, to reason with. On many occasions Daniel had to be escorted to the chaplaincy door because his behaviour was frightening other people in the building. He was, as many men of the road are, a little smelly and he carried most of his possessions in the pockets of the huge overcoat that he wore winter and summer. He had a small radio, a knife, a bit of loose change, a pen, and a notepad. Daniel always intrigued me. He was obviously well educated. He could quote Shakespeare and Wordsworth and Coleridge at the drop of a hat. He would talk about literature when he was able to and some of the students who were studying literature would say that he was quite insightful about why and how things were written. He fascinated me because he would never tell his story. Most of the time he wasn't capable of doing so, but when he was sober he would just smile when asked about his past and say, 'It's another world, my dear, another world.'

Eventually my tenure as chaplain to the University came to an end. It was time to pack up and move on to another way of living. I was appointed to a Parish. I had been ill with depression in the last couple of years at the Chaplaincy and I knew it was the right time to go. The day I was moving out of the Chaplaincy, Daniel stood at the door and watched as box after box of my possessions came out; books, records, CDs, clothes, furniture, all sorts of things. As the men were loading the last of it onto the van, Daniel looked at me with a grin and said 'We don't need much to survive, do we?' I have thought about that since he said it and I realise just how true it was.

We don't need that much to survive but usually we surround ourselves with so much that we never get near that truth. Our possessions can blind us into thinking that we need them, and probably that we need more of them. We don't realise just how little we actually do need. The Benedictines operate from a very sound principle: each year they go through their possessions and get rid of anything they don't need or haven't used.

When Jesus sent out the disciples in the Gospels he gave very specific instructions which were to be followed.

'Take no more than you need', he tells them. You and I are sent out in the same way those early disciples were sent out. We are sent out to proclaim the Good News of God's love and forgiveness for all people. We are called to help people to realise how close God's kingdom is to them. We are called, chosen to bring life, and Jesus says to us as he said to those first disciples, 'Do not take anything more than you need on your journey'. It seems to me that any metanioa experience has simplicity as one of its fruits. Simplicity of mind and heart and simplicity of need. It is one of the greatest signs to the world that God is alive and God is enough when we live simply. I often think to myself that it could well be that our witness to simplicity might well stop the world destroying itself.

What does it mean to live in simplicity of heart? A woman who has had a huge impact on my life is named June. She is one of the best examples I know of what it means to live in simplicity of heart. In worldly terms she has very little, no central heating, no car, no sky TV, no fine clothes. Her job is to look after an elderly man who at times can be very difficult and the money she gets just about pays her bills. June lives in this world filled with joy, delighting in every moment, weeping with compassion at times and dancing with delight at other times. All of it comes from an experience of God's love that has bowled June over and helped her to understand what life is

really about. June has had a metanoia experience. She
has turned around and faced the love of God and she
knows that love is enough for her. She doesn't mind that
some people think she's crazy. Love is enough. That
experience of love has meant that June has a heart
for others. She is not overly concerned with herself so
she has an ability to reach out to others and brings so
much peace into their lives. I often think of her when I
read the beatitudes and the line, 'Blessed are the poor in
spirit for they shall see God.' The 'poor in spirit' were the
anawim those who knew their need of God more than
anything else. Any real metanoia or turning around will
so fill our hearts with joy at the goodness of God that
God and God alone will fulfil our heart's desire for
love, for peace, for forgiveness, for mercy. Simplicity of
heart implies that you are willing to take the risk of
intimacy, of knowing and being known, of being
vulnerable and weak with God and with others if you are
to know how to share love and happiness. According to
the beatitudes you have to love enough to mourn, you
have to lay down your own desires to be peacemakers. You
have to be people of justice and integrity. You have to
share in the same sort of relationship as Jesus has with
the Father, a relationship of mutual giving. The one who
has simplicity of heart will proclaim the kingdom of
God because it flows from a heart full of love.

What about simplicity of mind? I don't know about you but my mind often races at a great rate of knots with all sorts of things competing for space. St Paul tells us in the first letter to the Corinthians that we should put on the mind of Christ. What was the mind of Christ like? It seems to me that when Jesus came out of his metanoia experience, which is captured in the stories of his baptism and temptation, that he had only one focus. That focus was the Kingdom of God and Jesus' whole life was spent trying to bring about that Kingdom of love, joy, healing, and peace. I think metanoia leaves you with a mind that is focused on that reality. You could call it singularity of mind. Some people call it religious mania but it is when your mind is focused on the Kingdom of God and not on anything else. It is not about becoming more Religious. The Church is to help us in our struggle to become kingdom-orientated but it is not the Kingdom. The more we enter into metanoia, this life-changing encounter, the more deeply our mind becomes focused.

When I was first ordained I lived in a Parish full of ordinary people who opened their hearts to me. In the main they were kind and warm and open and I loved being with them. Two of the people I met there were Margaret and Kevin. They were especially kind and their home became a place of refuge when I came home from school or had had a bad day. The kettle was always boiling and what ever they were doing stopped and I was welcomed. Kevin was a very quiet man but Margaret was quite the opposite. She was extrovert, dramatic, and full of fun and laughter. Margaret knew Jesus not just as a philosophy or a cerebral truth but deep in her guts. Jesus was life to her and she knew that without him she was nothing. Her metanoia had led her to a deep place of peace where the kingdom was her only focus and trying to make it real mattered more than anything else.

Margaret's life was an ordinary one. She had spent most of it in a small part of a small town apart from brief sojourn to London where she had hoped to become a professional singer. She returned from London, became a hairdresser and cared for her mum and dad for many years. Eventually, later in life, she married Kevin. She was very involved in her local Church. For years she was a member of the Prayer group, a reader, a member of the Scripture group, a helper with Baptism preparation. She was an avid campaigner and supporter of Christian unity and for years helped run a Christian fellowship group in her house before it was really acceptable. She was involved with Women Aglow and Women's World Day of Prayer. She was a woman of faith. Her encounter with Jesus touched the very fibre of her being. She loved Jesus and her relationship with him mattered more than anything. It allowed her to be loving and generous and warm. I benefited from her kindness more than most. Her relationship with the Lord enabled her to be vulnerable and even when she was hurt to bring that hurt before the Lord for healing. She was a brave woman who faced her own shortcomings and inadequacies with courage because she knew that was loved by God. You might say that you have met people like Margaret in every Church community. The difference was that it was all done to build the kingdom. She would endure anything for the sake of the Kingdom of God. She often said to me that without praying every day for the strength to build the kingdom her life would be empty and she would be nothing. She lived and died in simplicity of mind focused sharply on the Kingdom of God and love and life flowed from her.

When my mum was dying she was allowed to go home after four weeks in hospital. Nothing more could be done for her and she wanted to be at home. She lived for another four weeks and for two of those she remained in her own home. One day she asked me to walk around the flat with her and to write down what she told me.

She immediately began to pick up the things that had been very important to her during her life and she told me who she wanted to give them to. As she shared out her belongings I realised that they had become very

unimportant to her. What was of far more importance
was that through them she could share herself with
other people. At one point I asked her if it hurt to give
it all away. She said, 'No, it was only lent to me and it's
all for the good of others.' 30 - 1 · 15

For me, it was a real lesson in simplicity of need. 'We don't
need much to survive do we?' in the words of the wise sage
Daniel! The Kingdom of God is essentially about the
sharing of life and love with those around us. God's love
and goodness is to be shared through the way in which we
live. In Luke's Gospel we are told that the Pharisees who
loved money laughed at Jesus when he spoke of simplicity
of need. Even the good Religious people of the day had
not learnt that everything is gift and for the good of all. I
hope, as the good Religious people of today, we have
begun to learn the lesson but without metanoia I doubt it.
It is only an encounter with love that stops us short in our
tracks and turns us around that will stop the greed and the
need to possess that lies in the hearts of most human
beings. Nothing we have is ours alone. We are stewards of
what we have been given and it belongs to all. All
we have is to be shared; our lives, our time, our goods, and
our money. In being willing to enter into that sort of
experience we somehow enter the kingdom of God, which
is both a promise for the future and yet is in our midst. It
is only a real experience of the kingdom that satisfies;
nothing else will do it.

One of the challenges of Christianity is to put our trust not in the things around us but in the things of God. To put our trust in love and peace and to use what we have to make them more real. Metanoia turns us around and lets us know that trusting in God is all we need for a happy, fulfilled life. Yet so many of us seem to hold on to our possessions and make them our gods. We do it nationally, holding on to the power we have over smaller, less powerful countries. The refusal to write off the debts of so many countries, the immigration laws we have, the fear of different cultures, all increase the climate of fear we live in and the perceived need to protect ourselves at all costs. We do it as individuals. The new cars, the new kitchen, the rise in wages become everything to us. We hold on and we hoard and we don't look at the needs of those around us. We feel sorry when the pictures from some war-torn or famine-ridden country invade our televisions and we may well feel moved to give but we hardly ever give of anything more than our surplus to help. That's what angered the prophets so much, particularly Amos, the lack of real concern for the needs of others. Eventually that selfishness blinds us to the truth of God's kingdom and if we don't recognise the kingdom then we can't live in the kingdom.

Metanoia leads to simplicity. Encountering God in such a way that the very building blocks on which your life is based change, is to turn your life upside down and live in a radically different way. To live simply is the hope of the world. Without a joyful, contented witness to simplicity it could well be that the world will destroy itself, as richer nations do everything in their power to protect themselves against poorer nations. Pray for simplicity of heart, mind, and need, and with the Lord you will be co-operating in the salvation of the world.

CHAPTER SIXTEEN

JOY - A FRUIT
OF METANOIA

Part of the work I do involves spending time with people and listening to their stories. Last year I found myself in a retreat centre south of London listening to the stories of several religious sisters. Some of them were very sad to see the congregations that they had given their life to beginning to crumble around them. They saw dwindling numbers and communities full of elderly people. Some of them were fearful about the future. What would happen to those who needed nursing care when there was nobody left to do the caring? In many senses it was a depressing picture as these good women shared their concern and their sadness at what was happening.

It is a picture that is replicated all around us at the moment in the church. Life is changing. There are far fewer priests than there used to be. Indeed in the future there will be even less. Numbers are falling, our congregations are getting smaller and there is certainly more grey hair than anything else in the pews on a Sunday morning. People are deserting practices which seem to them to be irrelevant. Many of those who stay wonder why they are there but are afraid to desert what has been handed down to them. People are getting older and there seem to be very few new people around. It can be both discouraging and disheartening.

Let's get back to the retreat. One of the sisters came in to see me and told me a little bit about her life. She was ninety and had suffered from cancer twice and had just been told that it had come back and was untreatable. She told me that all her family were dead and she was one of seven sisters left in this country in her congregation. All the time she told me her story there wasn't an ounce of self pity or gloom to be seen. If anything, the opposite was true. A smile played around her lips and her eyes shone brightly. After listening to her story I decided to quicken the process and asked how she felt about the state of her congregation. She smiled at me and her eyes twinkled and she asked me why that particular question. I told her of the sense of sadness and despondency that I was picking up from some of the other sisters. She thought for a moment and then said that yes there was a great deal of dying happening but that death was the way to life and she just hoped that she would be around long enough to see the new life spring forth from the seeming death. As I listened to her I was filled with hope and I caught something of her joy so I asked her what it was that filled her with hope and joy. She said to me that she read the Scriptures every day and because of that she knew that from every death sprang new life.

The word of God had filled her with hope and joy. Metanoia was happening within her and so she was brimming with joy and it spilled over. It was catching. It was a joy that her life's situation and probably her forthcoming death could not take from her. That deep-rooted sense of joy is not the feeling of happiness that is here today and gone tomorrow. It is not that which is usually dependent on what is happening in our lives. Rather, it is that deeply-felt sense of joy that comes from outside ourselves. It is a gift and it is never shaken by the circumstances of life. It comes as a result of a metanoia experience and in many senses it is counter cultural. The world does not understand the sort of joy that comes from God. How can we be filled with joy in a world that is falling apart? How can joy be at the centre of our being when our lives are besieged by illness or bereavement or unemployment. How can joy well up within us when we are living in war torn areas? Joy is a gift, it is something given and we can know it in the depths of despair and the heights of happiness. It is an infilling that we experience when we turn around and face love.

One of my favourite quotations in the Scriptures comes from John's Gospel. 'I came that they might have life and have it to the full'. You could say that's all about going to heaven when you die or you could remember that Jesus was a Jew and that Jews are very much a present-moment people. When John has Jesus say, 'I came that you might have life and have it the full', it's about the here and now. John Main, the great practitioner of Christian Meditation said this about joy: 'Faith in the Kingdom of God is what makes us light of heart and what Christian joy is all about.' So, for John Main, Christian joy is all about the Kingdom of God. I have already written about the kingdom earlier in this book. Suffice to say that the kingdom that you find primarily talked about in Mark's Gospel is about fullness of life so this sense of joy and fullness of life are somehow intimately connected. If you are full of life you will be full of joy and if you are full of joy you will be full of life.

Of course metanoia is a process we enter into and its fruits are constantly being deepened and renewed. At times they have to be restored. A few years ago I was working with a group of religious sisters and during the time we were together we had periods of prayer. During one of them I invited the sisters to be still and allow the love of God to touch them. One of the sisters began to weep as she remembered an incident that had happened some thirty years before when one of her superiors had treated her very badly. It was stopping her opening up to love and had robbed her of her joy. She said afterwards she had always resented the woman and was very angry with her. That incident had coloured her perceptions and made her look at the order she was part of with jaundiced eyes. She looked at the world in the same way and yet this day as she faced the pain within her and began to weep, she began to experience within herself a real freedom. Love touched her. She wrote to me a couple of months later and told me that she had begun to see her Religious life in a new way and that she had even been to see the old woman who had been her superior and they had begged each other's forgiveness. She told me that her joy had been restored and a little like the Samaritan woman it was always bubbling up just below the surface.

The journey of metanoia will help us deal with the things in our lives that rob us of our joy so that we can become joy in a world that has lost its zest for life and simply lurches from crisis to crisis. Never let life rob you of the joy of being alive, the joy of knowing that God is with us. This process is not about doing anything, but more about becoming. It is about becoming love, becoming forgiveness, becoming peace, becoming joy, because that is what you have met in the heart of God. I heard someone say recently that as long as we do loving things and joyful things and peaceful things we are one step removed from the metanoia the Gospel calls us to, because it is all about becoming. We are to become joy.

I love the encounter between Jesus and the Samaritan woman in John's Gospel. It is so wonderful to see the woman's encounter with love and how it changes her. Let's go back a little in history. The Samaritans were almost like second cousins to the Jews but because there were cultural differences and religious differences the Jews refused to have anything to do with them. It was an antipathy that had its roots way back in Israel's history. After the reign of Solomon, Israel was divided into two kingdoms. Those in the Northern Kingdom integrated with the occupying Babylonians. There were marriages and relationships which in time gave birth to the Samaritans. Those who were left in the Southern Kingdom saw those in the Northern Kingdom as having compromised themselves and their God. The Jews would have nothing to with their neighbours and cousins and probably the same was true of the Samaritans, so Samaritans and Jews did not talk to each other.

Jacob's Well stands at an important crossroads on a very busy road. It had supplied life-giving water reaching back for generations and it was free. It was the place where people paused on their journey and rested so it was not unusual for people to stop and take a drink there. Let's pick up the story as John tells it in his Gospel. A woman goes for water at the well. As she approaches the well, the women sees a man there but she does not intend to get too close because she knows by the way he is dressed that he is not a Samaritan. I guess her plan was to help herself to the usual supply of water and move on. She is shocked embarrassed and scared when the stranger speaks to her. His accent confirms what his clothes had already suggested. He is not one of them. His request is simple. He asks her only for a drink. It is a simple request, but it throws her into confusion as she recognises this stranger as different. The Samaritan women, despite feeling uncomfortable, does not run away; she stays and enters a life-giving experience. Jesus gives her the opportunity to be who she was created to be, and in the middle of what is obviously a complicated messy life, Jesus quenched her thirst with life-giving water. What happened to her? She felt as though she had a fountain of living water bubbling up within her that she could not contain. Rekindled joy. When you encounter pure unconditional love you cannot fail but be filled with joy in response. That is what happened to the Samaritan woman. She entered into metanoia. She turned around and met that love that can sweep us off her feet and joy was the fruit of that experience. One of the beautiful gifts that comes from metanoia is always joy.

As I travel, I meet so many people who do not have real joy in their life. Their whole existence seems to be dominated by the need to keep on reflecting on the sin in their lives and in the lives of others in the hope that they might just be forgiven. I meet good people who think they are on fire with God who are negative, heavy, and unable to lift the gloom that follows them around. Whatever they are into, it is sadly not the Gospel because joy is central to the Gospel. At the moment, Pope Francis is always talking about joy. Just recently he wrote, 'The gospel joy which enlivens the community of disciples is a missionary joy.' In other words, the joy that we experience when we realise who God is and how much we are loved is to spill over from us and affect the lives of others.

This joy does not mean that those who experience such joy never have any sadness or pain in their lives. Even if their personal live are relatively free of such things they will inevitably feel the pain of the world as God feels it. They will be catapulted as Jesus was into entering the pain and suffering of those around them. Nor does it mean that we shouldn't acknowledge the feelings that usually accompany those realities it just means we know that beyond the pain that life sometimes brings there is joy always deep joy because when God gives a gift it is never revoked. Joy is a fruit of metanoia and once given it never leaves us despite what might be thrown at it. I have known depression and heartache and even when it has been at its worst I have never doubted that somewhere below the surface there is joy. It is that joy that can transform the world.

9 - 2 - 2015

CHAPTER SEVENTEEN

A BLESSING
FOR THE WORLD

About ten years ago a cousin of mine was dying with cancer of the liver. She was forty-four. I went to visit her about a fortnight before she died because she had asked to see me. I hadn't seen her since I was a child although I had heard a lot about her over the years. I knew that she was an artist and that creativity was very important to her. I had heard that she had tried acting for a while and that she had lived in France running a vineyard for some years. One of my cousins told me with a knowing look that she was quite bohemian in her attitudes and lifestyle and I didn't have the courage to ask what that might mean. I pulled up outside her house and I have to say I felt extremely anxious. I didn't know what she was expecting from me or why she had suddenly decided to see me. So it was with great trepidation that I rang the bell. After a few moments she answered the door and my fears dissipated. Just looking at this woman, I knew that here was someone who was brimming with life. It was attractive and compelling. Her eyes burned and sparkled within her thin face and her humour and directness shone out of her.

As I went into her house she told me that after an
hour with someone she got very tired and I would have
to leave when that happened. She then said something
that I hadn't expected. She looked at me full in the face
and said, 'We only have an hour and it is probably the last
hour we will spend together so tell me who you really are
because that is what really matters'. We could have wasted
the time talking about the past or maybe a bit about the
future. Instead we spent the next hour living each moment
laughing and crying and sharing very deeply about what
was going on inside of us. It was a very precious, very
real, time and somehow in that sharing I experienced
God incredibly powerfully. Life had moulded Jan into a
very real, vital, human being and her vitality was
infectious.

She said that when she was diagnosed with her cancer and
was told it was terminal, her mind went into overdrive. She
panicked about what the future would bring and who
would be with her when she died. She said that she
wondered whether the God she had learnt about in her
childhood would condemn her for the way in which she
had ignored God's ways. I guess that was to do with her
bohemian lifestyle. I never did discover what that was!
She decided that she would read the bible, go back to
Mass, anything that would help her discover who God is
and whether God was going to pay her back. It was all

to no avail. She said nothing happened and her mind continued racing. Then she said one day God found her. She couldn't explain how or why. She simply got out of bed one morning and she knew that she had no need to be afraid. Metanoia had happened and she was certain of only one thing, that God's love was enough to see her through life and death. It was extraordinary.

I will never forget Jan, who taught me how necessary it is wrestle with God and with ourselves in order to be led to that grace-filled moment, that moment of metanoia. In touching it we find ourselves and the God who lives deeply within us. In that metanoia we are turned around to see things differently and to know that love is enough. That is what fills us with life that is contagious and infectious. I am always aware that we only have the present moment in which to be open to metanoia but I don't always act as though it were all I had. We do not have yesterday or tomorrow, just this moment and it seems to me that the Gospel invites us to be open to the gift of meeting the Lord who is always present even when we are unaware of that presence. That is the transforming moment. That experience is metanoia. The moment of meeting is the one which revolutionises our inner being. That is when we are spontaneously living in the Kingdom of God. The Kingdom is not about the future, when we get to heaven, as so many of us seem to think it is. It is about the present moment and living that moment to the full even the moments that are sad and painful. That living in the moment is the blessing we have to share with the world and it comes about because of metanoia.

10-2-15

Another way of talking about metanoia is to talk of falling into grace. It is obvious to me as I travel around these islands that it is only when we turn around and fall into the reality of God's grace that we find true inner freedom. We cannot free ourselves much as we try with our self-help books and gurus who promise us liberty from every kind of addiction. Most of us, in fact I would go so far as to say all of us, are damaged psychologically, spiritually, and emotionally, to a greater or lesser degree. That is why we find it so difficult to live in the moment or to trust in the gift of now. It is why we try and control life rather than letting it unfold. It is why, so often, we miss the moment that can transform us. It is only the power of God washing over us that can enable us to turn around from that overpowering damage and stand vibrant and free. Grace, the unconditional love of God, is vital for human beings if we are to find life. Without it we become harsh, rigid, critical people who are always looking for someone else to take the blame for anything and everything. If you don't believe me then ask yourself the question why our newspapers and news programmes rejoice in stories about people who have fallen from their pedestal and are being held to account. Ask yourself why there are so many adverts on television where firms of solicitors promise huge amounts of money for accidents that happen. Our politicians, our celebrities, our clergy, all have to answer for their sins. Everything has become someone's fault. We have become a blame culture. Someone has to pay the price and so long as it is not me then I don't really care who it is. What a turgid, sad existence. I find it a real sadness that most human beings live in that sort of way.

I grew up in a house that was filled with the music of the 60's. My brother was seven years older than me and was a teenager when the Motown sound and the Beatles and, a little later, Simon and Garfunkel, captured the hearts and minds of young people everywhere. I was a little boy but loved, when I was allowed, to sit and listen to the music that he and his friends played. One of the songs which captured the whole of that time for me was by Simon and Garfunkel: 'The sound of silence'. It is a song that speaks of the darkness in the world. It's full of disillusionment about the way things are. There's a hopelessness in it but there's also a cry of 'if only.' If only we'd listen to one another properly. If only we'd really look at the injustice in the world. If only we'd build on the goodness that's in every person. If only we'd tear ourselves away from the Gods we've made of materialism and riches then maybe, just maybe, we'd begin to appreciate the beauty that's in the world and in every human being. Maybe then we'd begin to afford each individual the sort of respect and dignity they deserve. Maybe we would begin to understand what love means and what our destiny is about.

Jesus came to rescue us from the disillusionment that dogs us about the world and about ourselves, through metanoia. He came to free humanity from a disillusionment that makes us maintain the status quo by simply doing nothing to make a difference in the world. A disillusionment that stops us hoping that life will be different. I think that's the truth of John's Gospel when he tells us that God so loved the world... John wants us to know the reality of God's love for us and for the world and to show how faith in Jesus will lead us into it more deeply. That's his perception of reality, the only reality there is. The world is to be liberated and set free because of the presence of Jesus and we are do all in our power to make the world what God's awesome love wants it to be, but it will only happen when we enter into metanoia, when we fall into grace.

Not to enter into that process is to be condemned. Why? Because we will live in a false world dominated by self hatred, self-pity, selfishness, arrogance, and pride. That willingness to live the lie is what condemns us, rather than to live in justice, truth, love, and peace. God does not judge in John's Gospel. We judge ourselves by our failure to respond to Jesus, to respond to his call to really live. Not to live in life and love is to condemn ourselves to something that is less than life. We all do it. We compromise to make ourselves acceptable. We contribute to the sexism, racism, bigotry, homophobia, power-struggles that make our world the false place that it is or we take refuge in some false religion where we cocoon ourselves from the world and do nothing to make it better. Humanity destroys itself and the world that we live in and God weeps.

Those of us who are followers of Jesus have something incredible to offer the world. Metanoia can free us to live with hearts that are full of life vibrancy and vitality. The transformed heart and mind is free to rejoice in the gift of life. Falling into grace means that we can live always looking at the world and those who live in it with fresh eyes seeing and knowing the presence of God. It means there is no need to be afraid of otherness or difference. It means we don't have to live caught on the treadmill of our own feelings and our own understandings. We can live with broad horizons always looking beyond ourselves living in this world knowing that we are part of something bigger than ourselves.

14 -2 -15

We need metanoia. We need to fall into grace so that the world can see in us a way of life that is full of vigour and energy. So many of us have made God small and petty, spending so much time repenting for our sins and little time moving into the bigger picture of abundance and plenty that frees, heals, and transforms and becomes a blessing for the world. It is that place where we know, as Jan knew, that God has already done it. God has given Godself away. The love of God is poured out. We are forgiven, freed, saved. The heart of God is love flowing out and there is nothing we can do to earn it. If only we knew that to be true. Turn around and face it head-on and let it overwhelm you. Then you will be the greatest of evangelisers. You won't have to do anything but simply be overcome with grace. That means you will laugh more and trust more. You will not be afraid. You will be happy to be yourself, never trying to be anyone or anything else. You won't need the trappings of life to give you your identity, because God will have done that for you. You won't have to win arguments. You won't need to control anything; life will simply happen. You will live in this world delighting in the smallest child and be filled with awe and wonder at the created order.

John Shea, the great American story teller and theologian, once walked up and down the aisle in a hall where he was addressing a group. As he did so he looked at each various individuals and said, 'You are full of grace, but you don't know it'. Metanoia enables us to know that we are full of grace. You and I are created out of love, to be filled with the grace of God, so that we can be empowered to live a fully human life, a life that is vibrant and full, a life in which every moment has meaning, a life in which we have found the power to deal with what makes life less than it can be.

Wherever you are reading this book today, fall into grace. Stop trying and striving and let grace over-whelm you. Turn around and let the power of God fill you. Just by falling into grace you proclaim the kingdom because of what you become.

CONCLUSION

I was recently in Las Vegas on holiday. As I walked around I was mesmerised by the size of the hotels and the themes that they are built around. I loved the lights which made it seem like day all the time and the fountains which danced majestically to wonderful music. I was amazed to find people at slot machines at 8.30 in the morning. While I enjoyed the buzz and the experience it struck me how unreal it all was and how all of it was built to serve the great god Mammon and to exploit our perceived need for wealth and material goods.

I was reminded of the story of 'The Velveteen Rabbit' by Margery Williams and the question asked of the old skin horse in the nursery: 'What is real?' The answer given by the old nursery toy is that 'real' is when you have been loved, really loved, so much so that your joints grow slack and your ears get ripped and your eyes fall out but you don't really mind because love has made you real. There is a profound wisdom in the story, that love is the only authentic way to discover our own reality and everything else that we think might help pales into insignificance as we discover a life that is vibrant and fulfilling because of the power of love.

Most of my work these days seems to be about encouraging people to take the time and space to pray and reflect and allow God to work within us. Part of that process is always the difficult task of facing the things which control us. It's about looking at what motivates us and what at times threatens to engulf us. The more I talk to people, the more aware I am of just how much 'letting go' is part of the spiritual life. Many of us hold on to things that stop us seeing that love is the only way. We hold on to our resentment, our unforgiveness, our small mindedness, and our hurts that sour us and make us see the world through clouded eyes. Few of us are willing to recognise our self-centredness or the desire we have for power. We desperately search for acceptance from others and play games with ourselves and with them to make that acceptance a reality.

We con ourselves that we follow the Gospel but sometimes use it as a means of shoring-up our poor self image without allowing it to transform us. Most of us never quite manage to let go of control. We cling on to our own strength and our own capabilities so that even when we cry out to God for help we are still trying to sort things out for ourselves and we call all of this human reality.

This doesn't make us bad but we are created for more. Metanoia will lead us to the more. The deep discovery of love that knows no end is what makes us real. It is what turns our drab futile grey existence into vital pulsating life. God became flesh to show us what love is. Dare we open our hearts and minds to love that transforms and make us real? Take time each day to open yourself to God. Meet love and become love whatever the cost and know the truth that Jesus came that 'we might have life and have it to the full.'

Further copies of this book
and Fr. Chris' other books:
Love is the Key and
When Did we Stop Skipping?
are available from

Goodnews Books
Upper Level
St John's Church
296 Sundon Park Road
Luton, Beds, LU3 3AL

01582 571011
www.goodnewsbooks.net
orders@goodnewsbooks.net